CULTURE SHOCK!

SUCCEED IN BUSINESS

The essential guide for business and investment

Australia

**Peter North
& Bea Toews**

Graphic Arts Center Publishing Company
Portland, Oregon

Photo credits:
BHP Ltd: 47
David Gray: 12, 71, 107, 118, 203, 209
International Wool Secretariat: 14, 52
Michelle Coulter: 99, 180
Peter North: 54, 149, 194

This book is published by special
arrangement with Times Editions Pte Ltd
Times Centre, 1 New Industrial Road, Singapore 536196
International Standard Book Number 1-55868-414-X
Library of Congress Catalog Number 98-84831
Graphic Arts Center Publishing Company
P.O. Box 10306 • Portland, Oregon 97296-0306 • (503) 226-2402

Printed in Singapore

Contents

Acknowledgements

Thanks to
David Gray, Rod Nash, Rod Carruthers, Jingquan Zhang, John Pace, Dr Charles Price, Helen Smith, Celine Delacca, Eda Mrsnik, Elizabeth Hayes, John Herbig, Jackie Lacy, Michelle Coulter, Michael Coulter, Ken Dickson, Colin Enright, Anna Boland, Jim McCracken, Libby Hull, Professor Ian Lowe, Malcolm Davidson, Peter Lansell, Dr Owen Potter, Gary Lyons, Ernest Rodeck, Will Bishop, Tammy Sanders, Gwen Clarke, Phil Hannan, Shova Loh, Geraldine Mesenas and Harlinah Whyte.

Introduction

Australia's attractions to a prospective investor include a substantial domestic market, a sophisticated business community, a first class low cost physical infrastructure, a highly educated population, a supply of skilled labour, a stable political system and a government that encourages overseas investment.

In addition the country offers quality of life advantages.

In 1997, the Hong Kong-based research company, Political and Economic Risk Consultancy, asked 287 expatriate executives living in East Asian countries to compare the quality of life in 11 Pacific Rim countries. Included in the survey were nine Asian countries plus Australia and the United States.

Survey results rated Australia the top location in lifestyle and amenities, followed by Malaysia and Singapore. In individual categories, Australia was top in health-care, educational facilities, sporting and recreational amenities, and housing. The areas in which Australia failed to gain top rating were personal security— where it came sixth after Singapore, Japan, South Korea, Hong Kong and China—and the quality of night life—where the Philippines rated top.

Australia's lifestyle attractions are also recognised by nonbusiness groups. Asked why she had decided to move to Australia, an immigrant from Hong Kong replied "for the space, the privacy, the fresh air and the opportunities for my children".

Unspoiled bush land just outside cities, vast empty beaches, an abundance of recreational facilities such as golf courses, clean air and water, availability of a wide range of foodstuffs and restaurants are quality of life factors taken for granted by many Australians but noticed by visitors.

Geographically located within the world's fastest growing economic region and blessed with an abundance of natural resources, Australia is the location many businesses choose as their regional headquarters in the Western Pacific.

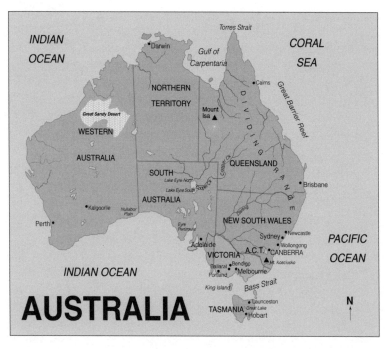

Map of Australia

CHAPTER 1

The Australian Economy

Australia—A Snapshot

Australia is the sixth largest country in the world and the only country to occupy an entire continent. The area of Australia (7,868,848 sq km) is about the same as the continental United States, excluding Alaska. Lying completely in the Southern Hemisphere, 40% of Australia's land mass is above the Tropic of Capricorn, with the balance in temperate latitudes.

Over 60% of visitors to Australia arrive from the north, from Asia or Europe, en route to cities such as Sydney, Melbourne, Brisbane, Adelaide or Perth. To reach their destinations in the south, the incoming travellers spend about three hours crossing the interior of the country. From a height of 10 km, a red-brown landscape of desert or semi-desert stretches to each horizon. In the Australian dialect of the English language, this featureless plain is known as the "outback".

The outback is flat, lightly vegetated and for the most part uninterrupted by man-made structures. Occasionally, a small town appears, or a mine site, or an isolated homestead belonging to an inland "station" as the huge grazing properties of the Australian interior are called. The commanding impression from the air is the miles upon miles of empty arid land. Australia is the driest inhabited continent on the planet. Only in the tropics, in Tasmania and on the coastal plains does rain fall in reasonable quantities.

Television series such as "Flying Doctor" portray Australia as a rural community full of pioneering people. While such historical role models still exist, they are a minority. Few people live in the outback. Far from its image as a rural community, Australia is one of the most urbanised countries in the world. Eighty-five percent of the population live in cities and towns of over 10,000 people.

Much of Australia is empty arid land. This featureless plain is known as the "outback".

Although the population of the country in 1996, at just over 18 million, suggests to some that Australia is underpopulated, much of the country is too arid for intensive settlement.

Australian Economy

The Organisation of Economic Cooperation and Development (OECD)[1] categorises Australia as a high income economy. Australia's quality of life indicators are close to OECD mean values. In 1996, Australian life expectancy was 77.6 years (OECD mean: 75 years). Telephone lines per 100 inhabitants was 49 (OECD mean: 49.7) while the number of cars per 1000 people was 444 (OECD mean: 374).

A substantial proportion of Australia's export revenues are derived from selling mineral and agricultural commodities to the rest of the world.

Brief Economic History

After the first European settlement in 1788, primary production was the country's most important economic activity. Initial agriculture was based on crops like wheat and corn brought from Europe by the first settlers. Later, livestock predominated. A few years after settlement, the first Merino sheep were shipped to the Australian colonies and did well in Australia's arid conditions—starting one of Australia's most important industries.

In 1820, the first bales of Australian-grown wool were shipped to the English port of Liverpool. For the rest of the 19th century, fast sailing ships, the Wool Clippers, circumnavigated the world from west to east, taking Australian wool to European markets.

From the 1850s until the mid-1870s, gold took over from wool as the colonies' principal export. Gold was discovered first in New South Wales, then in the Ballarat and Bendigo regions of Victoria. In 1852, a Victorian gold rush ensued on a similar scale to the 1849 gold rush of California.

By the 1870s, the Victorian goldfields were depleted of the easily-won surface gold. Wool then resumed its role as the premier export commodity, a pre-eminence that lasted well into the 20th century. The Australian colonies enjoyed collective prosperity, the economy riding, as the saying went, "on a sheep's back".

At the turn of the century, the Australian colonies were, collectively, the wealthiest per capita economy on the planet. Australia shared this distinction with Argentina, another sparsely populated country in the Southern Hemisphere, enriched by shipping agricultural staples to the European market.

In the 20th century, the Australian mining and mineral extraction expanded to include most of the minerals used in industry—coal, gold, iron, aluminium, copper, zinc, lead and nickel. In the 1950s and 1960s, the minerals industry boomed. Metal exports once more surpassed that of agricultural products.

In the first years of the 1970s, there was a short speculative boom in mining shares, particularly for those of nickel producers.

The Merino Sheep—the mainstay of 19th century Australian economy.

Shortly afterwards, the world entered a new era of declining commodity prices, a trend that has continued through the 1980s to the present.

Present Economy

The most frequently used measure of the relative wealth of nations is per capita Gross National Product (GNP). In the 1960s, most measures of this figure showed Australia to be one of the five wealthiest nations in the world. By 1980, however, the country's ranking in the *League Table of the World's Richest Nations* had declined to ninth.

Woven into so many of today's stories in the Australian financial media is a thread of concern about the country's economic performance. Many Australians are uneasy about perceived

OECD's Wealthiest Economies

	1996 ranking	1986 ranking	GNP per capita ($)
Luxembourg	1	4	32,206
USA	2	1	27,358
Switzerland	3	2	25,074
Norway	4	10	24,177
Iceland	5	9	23,576
Japan	6	13	22,919
Denmark	7	6	22,271
Canada	8	3	21,520
Belgium	9	15	21,446
Austria	10	12	21,367
Germany	11	5	21,083
Netherlands	12	14	20,621
France	13	8	20,510
Australia	**14**	**11**	**20,297**

Source: OECD Report, 1997.

Note:
1. All figures reflect real buying power (purchasing power parity).
2. Germany's decline relates to the fact that in the 1986 ranking, the figures only applied to West Germany. Its economic performance slowed down after the inclusion of East Germany.
3. Non-OECD economies whose 1996 per capita GNP exceeds Australia's include Singapore and Hong Kong.

economic problems—the continuing decline in per capita income relative to other countries, a persistent current account deficit and high unemployment. How to manage and arrest, and perhaps, even *reverse* the decline is relentlessly debated by all levels of Australian society.

The country is conscious of its geographical neighbours. Australia's position in the Pacific Rim, the domain of the Asian

Australia—A Statistical Overview

Population	18,060,000 (1996 census)
Land Area	7,868,848 sq km
Capital City	Canberra
Major Cities	Sydney, Melbourne, Brisbane, Perth, Adelaide, Canberra, Hobart, Darwin
Official Language	English
Literacy	97%
Life expectancy	76 years
Death rate	7 per 1000 population
Birth rate	13.7 per 1000 population

Economy

Unemployment	8.5%
Inflation	1.5%
GDP	A$478 billion (Current 1996 Prices)
GDP Growth Rate	2.6%
Private Consumption	A$314 billion (Current 1996 Prices)
Public Consumption	A$86 billion (Current 1996 Prices)
Gross Fixed Investment	A$100 billion (Current 1996 Prices)

Imports

Total Imports	A$77.8 billion
Major Imports	Manufactured Products
Major Trading Partners	USA, Japan, UK, Germany, New Zealand

Exports

Total Exports	A$76.0 billion
Major Exports	Agricultural and Mineral Products
Major Trading Partners	Japan, Korea, New Zealand, USA, China

Tigers, presents a blend of opportunity and threat that excites some Australians and concerns others.

Growth of the Australian Economy

The most frequently used measure of the economy's *vitality* is the growth of the GNP from one year to the next. This is the figure usually intended by economic commentators when they use the undefined term *growth* in conversations and articles about the economy. However, since the population base is also growing, the change of per capita GNP is perhaps a better measure of economic progress.

Australia's GNP Per Capita Increase

Year	Population increase (%)	GNP increase (%)	GNP per capita increase (%)
1950–1960	2.2	3.7	1.5
1960–1970	2.0	5.0	3.1
1970–1980	1.6	3.6	2.0
1980–1990	1.5	3.2	1.7
1990–1996	1.1	2.6	1.5

Note:
1. These figures are constant value dollars, adjusted for inflation.
2. Figures given include the average percent increase over previous decade.

Since 1950, Australia's per capita GNP has increased in real terms at about 2% per annum, similar to the United States for the same period but less than the global average of about 3%.[2]

Outlook for Growth

The Australian Bureau of Agricultural and Resource Economics (ABARE) issues yearly reports predicting the growth of the overall economy and its major sectors for the on-going five-year period. In its 1997 yearbook, ABARE estimated that the global economy will continue to grow into the early part of the 21st century, at an average annual rate of 3.7%, whereas average annual economic growth of GNP in Australia for the same period will be 3.5%.

Resources

By a measure of per capita resources, Australia is the wealthiest country on the planet. The country has huge quantities of minerals such as coal, gold, iron ore, bauxite, lead, zinc, copper, nickel and uranium ores. The only significant resource not in abundant supply is oil. In addition, Australia has vast tracts of agricultural land and as a consequence, is one of the world's leading producers of agricultural products, particularly wool.

Furthermore, the country's Economic Exclusion Zone (EEZ), defined by the 200 mile (321 km) limit from the coast, is the third largest in the world. Australia's EEZ is an additional area of 12,000,000 sq km—50% more than the country's land area—in which Australia has exclusive rights to explore, exploit and manage the resources of the sea and the seabed.

Trade

Since European settlement, Australia has been an exporter of commodities and an importer of processed goods. Within limits, this is still the trading pattern. Australia exports mainly commodities and imports mainly manufactured goods.

Nevertheless, manufactures is the fastest growing export sector. Substituting imported manufactures with local production is an important economic objective.

The importance of individual commodities in the country's trade has fluctuated over the years with commodity prices and customer demand. The single most important individual export in the 1990s has been coal (sometimes referred to as "King Coal" for its pre-eminence in the external account).

Australia's Total Exports, 1996–1997

Product	Value ($billion)	% Total Exports
Coal/Coal Products	7.8	10.2
Gold	5.6	7.4
Alumina/Aluminium	5.4	7.1
Iron/Iron Ore/Steel	4.6	6.1
Wheat	3.4	4.4
Wool	2.7	3.6

Source: ABS 1997 Yearbook

Note:
All figures are the sum of "raw minerals" and "processed minerals" in relation to each commodity. They include some of the amounts allocated to the "manufactures" section of the national accounts.

While Australia is still a dominant economic force in the region, the volume of trade relative to other countries has declined, particularly over the past two decades. From the viewpoint of trade, the diminished role of Australia in the world economy is more striking than the gentle decline of its GNP per capita ranking. From the 1970s to the 1990s, Australia's share of the total value of world trade declined from 3% to 1% despite an expansion of its trade in absolute terms during this period.

Since the fastest growing international trade sector was manufactured goods, trade by manufacturing economies such as Japan, Taiwan and Korea increased far more rapidly than Australia. Interestingly, Australia's trade is a smaller proportion of its GNP than most of its trading partners, belying a self-image that Australia is a particularly trade dependent nation. All nations trade, but Australia trades less than the average.

Terms of Trade

The Australian Bureau of Statistics compares the relative price of imports versus exports by computing a figure called the *terms of trade*—defined as the price of an average basket of the country's exports compared to the price of an average basket of its imports. Figures for the terms of trade for a 15-year period are shown below:

Terms of Trade	
	Terms of Trade
December 1982	96
December 1984	98
December 1986	82
December 1988	101
December 1990	94
December 1992	90
December 1994	92
December 1996	98

*Average July 1989–June 1990 = 100

Source: *ABS National Accounts, Standard 5206.0*, December 1996

While the terms of trade dipped in 1986 and again in 1993, by 1997, the figure had returned to its 1982 levels. In ABARE's view, the terms of trade are expected to peak in 1998, then decline through the remainder of the 1990s and into the first few years of the new century.

Volume of Trade

The growth of global trade in manufactured goods (6% per annum) is three times faster than the growth of trade in commodities (2% per annum). This has important implications for Australia. Since Australia imports more manufactured goods than it exports, the expanding trade in manufactures tends to increase the deficit of the current account. Australia's biggest current economic problem is the accumulated overseas debt resulting from successive years of current account deficits.

Australia's Trading Partners

For the first few years after first settlement in 1788, the British left the colony of New South Wales to fend for itself, visiting only irregularly to bring supplies and more convicts. Under British law, the British East India Company had a monopoly on trade with Asia, but the company initially showed little interest in the new Australian colony.

American Trade in the Colonies

Trading between the Australian colonies and the rest of the world started with America rather than Britain. In 1792, an American ship, the *Philadelphia*, was the first trading vessel from any country to reach Sydney.

Despite the East India Company's monopoly, Governor Phillip encouraged independent trade. He purchased the *Philadelphia's* entire cargo of rum, gin, tobacco, beef, pitch and tar.

By 1800, a total of 16 American trading ships had called. The first British mercantile ship did not arrive until 1807. Trade with American ships ceased after the outbreak of war between Britain and the United States in 1812 but resumed again in the 1820s.

During the 19th century, trade built up between the Australian colonies and both Europe and North America. The predominance of Europe and the United States as trade destinations continued until World War II. After the war, Asia became the focus of Australian trade.

The decline of the United Kingdom as an export destination for agricultural products accelerated in 1971 when Britain joined the European Economic Community (EEC)—later changed to the European Community or EC in 1993. Britain's membership in the EEC affected Australia's exports more than it did British imports into Australia.

Though Australia now exports the bulk of its commodities to Asia, it continues to import large amounts of manufactured goods from the EC and North America. As a consequence, Australia runs a trade surplus with Asia and trade deficits with Europe and the United States.

ABARE predicts that in the next few years, China is likely to become Australia's principal trading partner on both import and export accounts, and that the Chinese will be Australia's dominant trading partner for decades to come.

Trading Groups

To increase trade, an Australian national objective is to belong to whichever trading groups willing to accept its application for admission, particularly those in the Asia-Pacific region.

GATT The General Agreement of Tariffs and Trade (GATT)[3] Treaty was signed in Geneva in 1947 by the representatives of 23 nations. The objectives of the treaty were the expansion of world trade and the establishment of arrangements to settle disputes between trading parties.

In 1993, when the trading nations gathered in Montevideo for the Uruguay Round of GATT negotiations, the number of member countries had swelled to over 100. At the conference, the GATT Treaty signatories pledged to reduce tariff and non-tariff trade barriers.

After the Uruguay Round, Australia has played a leading role in the promotion of free trade, particularly by attempting to break into the protected EC agricultural markets on behalf of countries belonging to the Cairns group of agricultural producers.

Some exporters of manufactured goods claim that Australia is too enthusiastic about GATT, pointing out that most of its trading partners, while endorsing free trade principles in others, fail to practise the principles themselves.

Trade Associations in the Pacific Rim

From 1985 to 1995, the Southeast Asian Pacific Rim area was the fastest growing economic region in the world. Japan, Singapore and Taiwan were already mature economies while other Southeast Asian nations grew rapidly.

The 1997 collapse of the Asian economies was reported in the Australian press, which carried an article entitled "Troubles in Tigerland". Since the Australian economy depends greatly on exports to Asia, growth forecasts for the agricultural and mining sectors were greatly moderated in the second half of 1997.

Nations of the Pacific Rim have formulated a number of trade associations to which Australia has found itself, at best, a fringe member or a perpetual applicant. While making determined efforts to be accepted in Asia, Australia is still seen in some quarters as a European enclave, an ex-British colony that happens by some geographical accident to be located in the Pacific area. With the departure in 1997 of the British from Hong Kong, the only Western Pacific nations still administered by descendants of European colonists are Australia and New Zealand.

ASEAN The Association of Southeast Asian Nations (ASEAN) is the trade association in the Pacific area that Australia most yearns to join. Members of ASEAN—Brunei, Indonesia, Malaysia, Philippines, Singapore, Thailand, Vietnam—and those about to join—Burma, Laos and Cambodia—are nations on the Asian continent or nearby islands. Australia's—and New Zealand's—applications for membership of the association have so far been vetoed by Malaysia.

APEC The Association of Pacific Exporting Countries (APEC) is a broader based trade group than ASEAN. Its membership includes all the ASEAN countries plus Australia, Japan, Korea, United States, Canada, Hong Kong, Taiwan, Mexico, Papua New Guinea and Chile. APEC has a three-part agenda: trade liberalisation, trade facilitation and technical cooperation.

Bilateral Trade Agreement with New Zealand A special bilateral agreement—The Australia-New Zealand Closer Economic Relations Trade Agreement—has been concluded with New Zealand, whereby no tariffs are levied on goods traded between the two countries.

Currency—The Australian Dollar

Before Federation, and for a short while afterwards, Australian colonials conducted business in pound sterling. In 1913, Australia introduced its own currency, the Australian pound, which was initially valued at the pound sterling and later fluctuated, dictated by trading conditions.

Like the sterling, minor currency units of the Australian pound were shillings and pence. In February 1966, the currency was decimalised using ten shillings as the basis for the new currency. A national competition was conducted offering a reward for the citizen who could suggest a suitably dignified name for the new currency unit. After considering and rejecting offerings such as the *quid*, the *royal*, and the *kanga*, the authorities retained their prize money. For want of a better name, the new currency was christened the *Australian dollar*, with the *cent* as the minor unit.

After decimalisation, the exchange rate of the dollar was fixed at a daily meeting of the Board of the Reserve Bank of Australia (RBA), which is Australia's central bank. However, by the 1980s, financial controls were easing and currency markets were expanding. In 1984, the recently elected Labor government decided to float the currency so that its value in terms of other currencies would be set by market forces.

The value of the Australian dollar is most commonly stated against the US dollar in the daily press. However, a more meaningful measure is the *Trade Weighted Index* (TWI), which as its name suggests, is the value of the currency measured against a weighted average of the currencies of trading partners. The TWI is based on a rating of 100 in May 1970.

The following table shows that the value of the currency has drifted down slightly over time, demonstrating a weak correlation with the terms of trade.

Changes in Value of the Australian Dollar

Year	TWI	Terms of Trade	Year	TWI	Terms of Trade
1982	88	96	1990	58	94
1983	78	98	1991	60	94
1984	79	98	1992	55	90
1985	65	89	1993	51	88
1986	56	82	1994	53	92
1987	57	90	1995	55	95
1988	60	101	1996	58	98
1989	59	100			

Source: ABS 5206.0, 1996

Future Value of the Currency

The future performance of the Australian dollar has been notoriously difficult to predict. Each year, the Australian press invites economists working for a great number of banks, financial institutions and government bodies to forecast the dollar's value for the year ahead. The economists' predictions are printed in the newspapers, then assessed at the end of the prediction period.

Over the years, estimates have varied greatly and results have often been well wide of the mark. Predictions tend to be overwhelmed almost immediately by unexpected economic and political events.

In its 1997 issue of *Outlook,* ABARE reviews prospects for currency levels for the next five years. ABARE estimates that the value of the currency will slowly decline due to an expected easing of the terms of trade. ABARE estimates that the TWI in the period, 1997–1998, will be 57 and that this will decline progressively to a value of 53 by the year 2002.

Domestic Savings and Investment

In the mid-1970s, Australians were amongst the thriftiest people in the world, setting aside about 10% of GDP as savings. However, in the 1980s, the savings rate declined to about 6% and by the mid-1990s, to 3%.

The government saw two problems with the low rate of savings. Firstly, the country did not generate the development capital it needed. Secondly, the country faced the impending prospect of an ageing population unable to fund its own retirement.

In 1992, compulsory superannuation was introduced to address these twin concerns with a single measure. Labour unions agreed to forgo cost of living pay increases in return for receiving superannuation entitlements that could be cashed in later years. Employers were obliged to contribute a percentage of the employees' wages directly to a superannuation fund operated on behalf of the employee. Initially, the rate of employer contribution to these schemes was 4% of wages and salaries per year. The rate has been successively increased over the years, with a target of 9% to be reached in the year 2002.

Employer-funded superannuation thus represents a significant cost for foreign investors setting up business ventures in Australia.

The Balance of Payments Problem

Rapidly increasing mineral exports kept the current account in surplus in the late 1960s and early 1970s. However, a coincidence of adverse economic circumstances—a decline in the terms of trade, sluggish global economic growth and surging imports— produced a series of current account deficits in the late 1970s and early 1980s.

By about 1985, the accumulated overseas debt had increased sufficiently to attract media attention outside the financial pages. The national debt became a topic of conversation in the street. After the Australian Bureau of Statistics (ABS) computed the previous month's current account deficit, the treasurer would call a press conference and reveal to the hushed gathering "the figure". At this point various degrees of bedlam would ensue in financial markets, depending on how the figure announced performed against market expectations.

With widespread concern about the balance of payments, the value of the Australian dollar plunged in the first half of 1985, and continued to diminish through the balance of the year and into the next.

Some of the more pessimistic financial journalists, accustomed to writing in evocative terms, predicted a currency "melt-down" similar to Argentina or the Weimar Republic in Germany in the 1920s. The melt-down did not occur. The RBA increased interest rates and currency speculators moved in to support the dollar. Far from a collapse, the Australian dollar, when measured as the sum of interest earned and capital gained, was the top earner of the world's major trading currencies during the remainder of the 1980s.

Due to high real interest rates applying to Australian dollar deposits since the early 1980s, the currency has attracted more than its fair share of attention from currency traders. Despite the Australian economy accounting for only about 1% of world trade, the Australian dollar has, in the 1980s and 1990s, been the world's sixth most actively traded currency at times. In 1996, the daily average trade in Australian dollars was A$52.196 billion. This amount is approximately 200 times greater than the amount needed to sustain import/export operations. Most of the trading on the currency is short term investment.

The high level of interest in the currency by speculators tends to destabilise the dollar in relation to other currencies, making it prone to large fluctuations in value. Over the second half of the 1980s and through the 1990s, the Australian dollar has been the world's most volatile actively traded currency, along with the New Zealand dollar.

Keating's "Banana Republic"[4]

In May 1986, on a Sydney talkback radio station, the then treasurer, Paul Keating, remarked that Australia risked becoming a "Banana Republic". When the remark hit the Reuters screens moments later, the dollar dropped 5%. As its value fell to near 60 US cents, the wags of the financial press nicknamed the Australian dollar the "Pacific peso", after the currency of Mexico which was also in crisis at the time.

After the "Pacific peso" became a daily topic of conversation, the financial pages of *The Australian* newspaper ran a cartoon series spread over some months, featuring Keating wearing a sombrero and riding a mule through the cactus-studded desert of his bankrupt country, pausing now and again to chat to some passing derelict about the price of bananas.

The Australian dollar reached its lowest ever point of 57.2 US cents by 11 a.m. on 20 July 1986. By 4 p.m. the same day, the currency had recovered to 63.2 US cents, a testament to its extraordinary volatility at that time.

The RBA has, from time to time, tried to reduce this volatility by conducting "smoothing" operations: the bank itself entered the currency market to buy on the lows and sell on the highs. Although stabilising the currency was the main objective, these operations have been highly profitable for the bank and the Australian taxpayer. Buying currency on the lows and selling them on the highs was so successful that in the period, 1986–1990, the RBA's currency operations contributed $2.4 billion windfall profits to the beleaguered balance of payments.

Current Account Deficit

The merchandise and service accounts have been, more or less, in balance for most years. However, the legacy of overseas debt from accumulated current account deficits of previous years must be serviced by interest payments or dividend remittals. The net income balance in the table below is approximately equal to the entire current account deficit, which has been financed by borrowing money from foreign lenders and selling assets to foreign buyers. This shows up as "Net Foreign Liabilities" on Australia's national accounts.

Net Foreign Liabilities

Year	Liabilities ($billion)	GDP ($billion)	Debt/GDP (%)
1990–91	191	379	50.3
1991–92	200	387	51.8
1992–93	218	406	53.7
1993–94	238	430	55.4
1994–95	261	456	57.3
1995–96	285	486	58.6

Source: *International Investment Position*, Australia, June Quarter 1996 (ABS 5306.0)

Note:
1. Figures are at constant 1989–1990 prices.
2. The term *Liabilities* is defined as net debt plus net equity.[5]

Government Action on Australia's Balance of Payments Problem
Concerned about the long term risks presented to Australia by its international trading position, the federal government in the mid-1980s sought a way out of the debt cycle. Recognising that the fastest growing sector of international trade was manufactured goods, the government took steps to encourage manufactured exports. The government introduced initiatives through a combination of direct financial assistance, product development schemes, export incentive schemes and taxation incentives.

The policy appeared to bear fruit. Between 1990 and 1995, the value of manufactured exports grew by 106%—about double that of the global average for the period. Only eight of the world's 40 largest manufacturers increased their manufactured exports at a faster rate. For the six-year period, manufactured goods became the fastest growing category of Australian exports.

However, a change of government in 1996 brought changes to industrial policy, favouring the agricultural and mining sectors at the expense of the manufacturing sector. The incoming government's wanted to curb its expenditure deficit rather than continue to tackle the current account deficit. It also appointed a cabinet, comprising a significant minority of farmers who were inclined to pursue policies favouring primary industries.

The new government thus unravelled most of the export initiatives its predecessor had taken. As a result, the rate of growth of manufactured exports slowed in the first half of 1997.

Foreign Investment in Australia
Since Australia's persistent current account deficit must be financed by overseas money, foreign investment is absolutely essential to providing the working capital to keep the country going.

Minimum barriers to foreign ownership of business are imposed. Foreign investors to Australia will find that investment conditions are decidedly liberal. The degree of foreign ownership in Australia is high, and it is rising. Between the years of 1992 and

1995, the proportion of equity held by nonresidents of Australia to total commercial equity on issue rose from 25% to 30%.

The Currency Risk

Anyone who invests in a foreign country takes a currency risk. Most economists believe that a nation must balance its receipts and its expenditures over the long term in order to maintain a stable economy. As we approach the 21st century, prospective investors in the Australian economy should be aware that Australia's unresolved balance of payment problem may present a long-term threat to the value of the dollar.

On the other hand, a small school of Australian economists claim that as long as the exchange rate is free to find its level in the market, the level of debt does not matter as in Australia's case, where the majority of the debt is not in public hands.

Unemployment

The Australian Bureau of Statistics measures unemployment according to an internationally accepted definition of the International Labour Organisation (ILO). According to this definition, the unemployed include people who are actively seeking work as well as those who do not currently work for more than one hour per week.

Unemployment in Australia has increased over the years, hovering between 8% and 9%. Along with this increase is the increased dependency on social welfare. In 1973, the number of people on social welfare in Australia was 12.5% of the population (not all related to unemployment). By 1996, this had risen to 23%, 9% of whom were on unemployment benefits.

Some economists argue that the "real" unemployment is more likely to be around 15%. Included in the notion of real unemployment are people that have part-time work but seek full-time jobs, and people who want jobs but have become too discouraged to look for work. However, statistics show that the average number of hours worked per week has not changed significantly in 15 years[6], disproving the view that full-time work has declined.

Many economists perceive unemployment as a problem to which there is no solution. Jobs that once existed have disappeared through industrialisation. Computerisation—the second wave of automation—is wiping out entire career paths. At the same time, manufacturing and processing industries are under constant pressure from developing countries that have very low labour costs

Myths and Self Delusions

The Australian media has done the country a disservice by peddling a number of myths that are often accepted without question by many Australians. You may often encounter these myths in newspaper articles and normal conversation. A few of the better known myths are summarised in the following table.

The Facts of Myths

Myth   The Australian workforce is highly paid.
Fact   It costs more to hire a process worker in US, Japan, Korea and Germany—Australia's major trading partners.

Myth   Transport costs make Australia uncompetitive.
Fact   A KPMG survey shows that Australian transport rates are competitive.

Myth   Australian business costs are high.
Fact   Costs of rental, utilities and general living are amongst the cheapest in the world.

Myth   The Australian economy is dominated by mining and agriculture.
Fact   The combined output of mining and agriculture is 6.6% of GDP*.

Myth   Australian workers are recalcitrant at work and often organise strikes.

Fact   Australian workers are highly skilled, highly motivated and rarely organise strikes.

Myth   The Australian industry cannot compete because the domestic market is too small.

Fact   The Australian market is larger than the domestic markets of competing countries like Malaysia, Singapore, Hong Kong, Thailand, Switzerland and Sweden. The market for Australian products is the entire world.

*This figure as reported by the Commonwealth Statistician does not include downstream value-added operations such as steel making, aluminium smelting or food processing.

CHAPTER 2

Market Opportunities

General Trade Environment

In its endeavours to foster exports and thereby relieve the balance of payments problem, Australia has become acutely aware of the importance of trading with the rest of the world. As such, increasing exports is a constant political imperative. Australian politicians tirelessly travel overseas with entourages of business people to promote trade.

Despite the risk of exacerbating both the balance of payments problem and domestic unemployment, the government has not acted to stem imports. The government's free trade commitments to the World Trade Organisation (WTO) is the guiding economic principle on the external account. As a result, import tariffs have been progressively reduced since 1975. The government hopes that the competitiveness of Australian manufacturers will be increased by exposing them to the cleansing forces of global competition. On the other hand, as the manufacturing sector points out, an equally likely outcome of the government's tariff policy is that global competition could force them out of business.

Unlike most of Australia's major trading partners, few non-tariff barriers are imposed on imports into the country. Until recently, import quotas were imposed on goods like footwear and textiles to protect the local industry. However, quotas for all categories of goods have now been eliminated. No special design standards apply for imported goods except goods like cars, for which local specifications apply. Trade with Australia is thus encouraged or enabled, whether it be investment in the local economy or trade through imports or exports.

Compared to most countries, there are few restrictions on foreign investment. Export and import of capital is virtually unimpeded, as is repatriation of dividends and transfer payments. Foreign equity content is only restricted in a handful of industries, such as the ownership of media outlets.

Although joint venturing between domestic and foreign companies is common practice, there is no stipulation that foreigners should involve local equity partners in their Australian businesses. In fact, the Australian public sector is in the process of divesting of its ownership mostly to foreign owners, even in strategic industries such as electricity generation and supply. Privatisation of existing publicly-owned corporations has recently become a major business opportunity for overseas investors.

Business Privatisation

Businesses privatised in the past ten years include Commonwealth Bank, Australian Airlines, Qantas Airways, state-owned electricity companies, state-owned water boards, state-owned railways and suburban bus routes.

Businesses that may be privatised in the future include Telstra (the major telecommunications company), electricity, gas and water utilities, railways, some sections of the Australia Post (the postal service) and the Australian National Line (ANL), the coastal shipping line.

Making Contact

Australians are used to dealing with people at a distance and face-to-face meetings are not important to them. On its island continent of vast distances and few population centres, isolation has historically been a cultural reality. The majority of Australians are accustomed to doing business with people they have contacted only by mail or telephone.

There are also economic deterrents to meeting up with your far-flung business partner. Air travel within the country represents a significant business expense and is time-consuming. Though nothing beats a personal introduction, those wishing to trade with or invest in the country should not feel inhibited about establishing initial written or telephone contacts with Australian prospects from their own country.

Austrade

The Australian Trade Commission (Austrade) is a section of the Australian Department of Industry, Science and Tourism. Its principal function is to promote the export of Australian-made products. To this end, Austrade operates a database of existing and expectant Australian exporters and their products, which can be accessed on the Internet through "Austrade World Direct". Alternatively, the local office of Austrade will pass on trade enquiries to the relevant Australian business through one of almost 100 offices that it operates in 67 countries.

Austrade also coordinates displays for Australian exporters at a range of industry-specific trade fairs around the world like:

- Information Technology: CeBIT, Hannover
- Hospitality and Catering: Hofex, Hong Kong
- Education: Gulf Education, Dubai
- Building and Construction: Sibex, Singapore

This list is far from exhaustive. Enquiries can be made via the local Austrade office.

Austrade also provides information to foreign investors wishing to undertake projects in Australia.

Other Agencies

In addition to Austrade, which is a federal agency, the individual states of Australia maintain separate trade representatives overseas. Their purpose is to promote industrial activity within each particular state. For instance, all the six states maintain separate offices in addition to the federal consulate office at Australia House in London's Strand. Details about the location of particular state information offices may be obtained from Austrade. Alternatively, all state business ministries publish a web page that includes information about state business development offices.

Feasibility Studies

Feasibility studies estimating the anticipated economic returns of the project are a sensible precursor to any decision to commit investment funds into a project. While market survey and cost information could be painstakingly collected by the prospective investor, local help may speed up the process and produce a more accurate result. Australia offers an entire industry of consultants in management and other disciplines to analyse and provide all information needed.

Sources of Market information

Australian Bureau of Statistics (ABS) is the primary source of statistical data for the country. A statutory office run by the federal government, ABS issues a broad range of general statistics relating to Australia's macroeconomy, including detailed information about all sectors. Broad-based statistics such as inflation, unemployment and balance of payments figures are issued monthly while other information can be obtained annually.

Although the ABS publishes a large number of reports, finding the statistics you require need not be an onerous task. ABS publishes a yearbook with aggregate data on all aspects of the economy. This is available in printed form and on CD-ROM. ABS data is generally free of charge—except for published works for sale—and may be obtained either over the phone, by Internet or through the ABS office and library in the capital city of each state.

Information of a more specific nature is available from sources such as industry groups. For instance, the car industry publishes monthly car sales figures according to manufacturer and model.

In addition, the prospective investor can refer to a large number of specialist trade publications produced in Australia.

An increasing number of Australian companies have their own web pages on the Internet. The more traditional modes of making contact are the *Yellow Pages* phone book or the international *Kompass* buying guide.

Besides information that is commercially available, most foreign governments can provide helpful information through their own trade consulates in Australia.

Industry Networks
Numerous networks and lobby groups exist to promote the interests of particular industry groups. They can be contacted for information and assistance. Broad-based networks cover industries like agriculture, minerals, manufacture, retailing and tourism, as well as more specialised segments such as forestry, metal trades and small businesses.

Industry Associations
Industry networks exist to support most products and activities. The following is a sample of a few of the major industry associations in Australia:

Agriculture: National Farms Federation
Minerals: Australasian Institute of Mining and Metallurgy
Manufacture: Australian Chamber of Manufacturers
Retailing: Retail Traders Association of Australia

A comprehensive list of industry networks can be easily obtained through advisory services such as Austrade and business assistance bureaux in the various states. Alternatively, the company, Information Australis, prepares a *Directory of Associations* with a comprehensive list of all special interest groups in Australia, including company names, addresses, office bearers and contact details. In its 1997 issue, this directory had over 7,000 entries.

Ethnic Networks

New settlers in Australia have been encouraged to maintain their cultural identity while at the same time coexisting within the Australian society. As a result, virtually all nationality groupings maintain active societies, which provide information and other assistance to prospective investors. While these groups primarily pursue social rather than industry objectives, they are worth contacting for assistance and business networking. Such networks exist for virtually every ethnic group in Australia.

Business Networks

A primary source of business information in Australia is the Australian Institute of Management (AIM). Area-based business networks also exist, which promote the interests of small business—predominantly retail. Promotions are made within particular geographic areas—in the case of cities, a group of suburbs, and in the case of country areas, entire towns.

International charity-cum-business organisations such as the Rotary Club and the Lions Club are well-represented in Australia. Special groups also exist for women in business. Representatives of big business usually gather in exclusive businessmen's clubs like the Sydney Club, the Melbourne Club, and the Australia Club.

Business Agents

There are some advantages in taking over an existing business rather than forming a new one from scratch. A minor industry of business agents exists to assist those who wish to buy and sell existing (mainly small) businesses. Both the prospective vendor and purchaser of the business register with the agent. If the sale of a business is effected in this way, the business agent receives a commission from the vendor in the same manner as a real estate sale. A list of business agents can be found in the *Yellow Pages*.

Imports

Australia is a large and growing market for overseas exporters. Merchandise imports into Australia totalled A$79 billion or about 17% of GNP in 1996. The average annual rate of increase of imports for the period, 1982 to 1996, was 7.5%.

Australia is one of the easiest countries into which to import. No import quotas exist on any category of goods. In general, non-tariff barriers to imports—compliance with local standards, special rules about packaging, etc.—are minimal.

However, certain imports are restricted as detailed in the Customs (Prohibited Imports) Regulations. Under the various schedules in these regulations, a small number of goods are banned entirely while other goods cannot be imported without written permission from the Australian Customs. In general, restricted or banned goods are those that present some danger, such as military hardware, drugs or goods with poisonous surface treatments.

Prohibited Imports
Under the 1997 amendment to the Customs (Prohibited Imports) Regulations, the only goods specifically prohibited (under schedule 1 of the regulation) are:

- Any goods bearing the name "Anzac"
- Four particular breeds of dogs (one being the American Pit Bull Terrier)
- Matches containing red or yellow phosphorous

Permission for the import of all other goods can be applied for (though not necessarily granted). The import of goods from certain countries such as Iraq and Libya is also restricted or banned.

Source: Australian Customs Service

As an island continent, Australia has developed unique flora and fauna that are particularly susceptible to the depredations of imported species. After several disastrous experiences with imported exotic species now feral and out of control in the country, such as cane toads, rabbits, foxes, cats, goats, thistles and brambles, Australian authorities try to avoid the entry of exotic living things into the country, whether they be bacteriological, vegetable, animal or insect. Interiors of passenger planes are sprayed with insecticide upon arrival in the country. Organic products, such as leather and bamboo that may carry insects, must be treated in an approved manner before they can be imported. Likewise, organic packaging material must be chemically treated to eliminate the possibility of pest infestation.

Goods bearing trademarks similar to the registered trademarks of locally produced goods may also be classified as prohibited imports. But the Australian Customs Service will only act on the initiative of the local trademark owner. The trademark owner may be deterred from legal action, which entails the arduous and costly tasks of registering the objection, and then proving the case.

Domestic Attitude to Imported Goods

In this age of globalisation, goods from most parts of the world can be found on the Australian market. For fast moving products such as household items, toys and the like, consumers are not generally concerned about their country of origin. For consumer durables and industrial products, however, the country of origin may influence the buying decision.

Products from different countries are perceived to have different quality standards. North America, Japan, Scandinavia and most countries in Europe are considered to make goods of top quality. China, Taiwan, Korea and the other Asian Tigers have improving reputations. Eastern European products still have to live down past reputations for poor quality while South American and African products are not widely known.

For a brief period in 1995, Australian consumers mounted effective boycotts against French products in protest of France's nuclear testing in the South Pacific. This antipathy has since died a natural death. No other country in the past 10 years has attracted blanket disapproval for political reasons.

Domestic Attitude to Local Goods

Australians have somewhat ambivalent perceptions of the quality of goods produced in their own country. For a long time, the Australian Federal Government promoted an active "Made in Australia" campaign, where local goods carried an identifying logo to authenticate their domestic origins. Goods were labelled "Made in Australia" or "Australian made", and carried an identifying sticker in the national colours. This campaign was scrapped in 1996—along with many other initiatives of the previous government—as the incoming government tackled its inherited budget deficit. What effect, if any, the "Made in Australia" campaign had is hard to say. The rules defining local manufacture were difficult to define and control.

Exports

While exporting is encouraged, export of some goods is restricted, as are some export destinations. Restrictions of exports are detailed in the Customs (Prohibited Exports) Regulations, which can be obtained from Australian Customs Service (ACS). Goods on which export restrictions apply can be exported if written permission is obtained from the ACS. Such goods include specified drugs, specified wildlife, blood products, military equipment and minerals like alumina, bauxite, coal and liquid petroleum gas. Restricted destinations include countries such as Iraq, Rwanda and Yugoslavia.

Some exported goods are eligible for an export concession called *drawback*—a reimbursement of any import duty, excise and sales tax paid on goods being exported or re-exported. Information on rules relating to drawback can be obtained from ACS.

Export Finance and Insurance

Export Finance and Insurance Corporation (EFIC) is a federal statutory corporation established to insure Australian export businesses against nonpayment by overseas buyers. The price of this insurance is about 0.7% of the invoice value. The EFIC can also assist in arranging finance for exporters.

Marking and Packaging

Australian Customs has rules specifying minimum standards for the marking of packages. The Commerce (Trade Descriptions) Act 1905 specifies the packaging and marking regulations of imported and exported goods.

Packaging and Marking Regulations
Under the regulations, the following information must be displayed on the packaging of goods:

- Nature, number, quantity, quality, purity, class, grade, measure, gauge, size or weight of the goods
- Country in which the goods were made or produced
- Identity of the manufacturer or packager of the goods
- Method of manufacturing or preparation of the goods
- Materials from which the goods are composed
- Existing patent or copyright that goods are subject to (if any)

*Markings must be in the English language

Prepackaged goods, defined as "goods normally sold in the packages in which they are imported", must be marked with at least the country of origin and the material composition, both on the product itself and the packaging. In addition, the marking or labelling must be in a prominent location. For example, a label sewn on the collar of a shirt satisfies marking regulations whereas a label sewn into the inside of a pocket or into a seam of the garment does not.

Location

While Australians consider the distance from foreign markets an impediment to the development of local industries, the domestic market itself is not insignificant. The GNP of Australia is comparable to that of Korea and Taiwan. In addition, the country is geographically situated in the fast growing Pacific Rim area. Many businesses, particularly those from the English-speaking world, have established their regional headquarters in Australia.

Manufacturing Sector

Manufacturing in Australia has had a checkered history. For much of the 19th century, Australia prospered from its primary products of wool and gold. The country was blessed with such an abundance of physical assets that selling what could be grown or mined seemed liked an effortless pathway to wealth. To some, this still seems the way. Though manufacturing is the largest sector in the economy outside the service industry (in dollar terms, manufacturing is five times the size of agriculture and over three times the size of mining), the government's attention to its needs has been sporadic at best, and neglectful at worst.

A Critique

"Many people in Australia think the manufacturing industry should be regarded with suspicion. That we should be content to herd sheep or milk cows. Why should we disturb the bucolic peace of our community with factories when we can get our goods made in Germany?"

— Octavius Beale, President of the Manufacturers' Association, 1880

Manufacturers today might claim that one hundred years later, the attitude articulated by Octavius Beale has not changed. Such is the combined influence of the agricultural and mining lobbies on public and political opinion that many in the wider community still regard the country as a mere commodity exporter that practically imports its entire requirement of manufactured goods.

This is another of the country's economic myths. In fact, as measured by the ratio of manufactured imports to domestic consumption of manufactured goods (a ratio termed *import penetration* by OECD), Australia imports a lower proportion of its manufactured goods than industrial heavyweights such as Germany, France and the United Kingdom.

Manufacturing in Australia started with the first settlers. At the time it was formed, the colony of New South Wales was as far away from the workshops of the world as it was possible to be. The British Government expected the colonists to fend for themselves. However, by the end of 1788, the first year of settlement, the colonists were running their own brick and tile factory and making their own cloth. They had also built a 10-ton vessel for work on the Parramatta River. The colony was aiming to become self-sufficient in manufactured goods as fast as it could.

Later, when the wool trade was developed with Europe, a greater volume of manufactured imports flowed in. Manufactured products were shipped to Australia both as backload cargoes and as ballast for the otherwise empty clippers on their voyages south.

According to economic historians, there was a time (from 1880 to 1890) when Australian labour productivity, as measured by output of manufactures per hour of labour input, was the highest in the world—50% higher than the United Kingdom and the United States.

During World War II, Australia's supply lines to its allies were cut off by the German and Japanese navies, and the country was forced to cope on its own. Local industry boomed and the country became self-sufficient in many of the things it now imports, for instance, machine tools and aeroplanes, as well as the full range of military equipment.

The end of the war saw the resumption of commodity exports and the gradual decline in industry. Local manufacture of goods were not a high priority when booming commodity exports generated the foreign exchange to purchase manufactured goods from more industrialised countries.

For much of the 20th century, the manufacturing industry was sheltered by high tariff barriers, which in the mid-1960s averaged 35%. In comparison, the tariffs in the mid-1990s averaged 4%. Today, the lowering of tariffs and globalisation has made Australia's manufacturing industry world competitive. Though sections of the Australian manufacturing industry are under pressure from imports, Australian manufacturers have found ways to compete in regard to both price and quality.

Government support has been sporadic; the manufacturing industry lacks the powerful lobby groups of mining and agriculture. There is no long-term industry plan comparable to countries of comparable or smaller populations like Malaysia, Singapore, Switzerland and Sweden.

During the mid-1980s, the government developed initiatives to raise the export performance of the manufacturing industry, with spectacular results. In the period, 1990 to 1995, the export of manufactured goods rose by an average annual rate of 15.6%. However in 1996, in an attempt to address its budget deficit, the incoming Liberal government withdrew some of the incentives to manufacturing instituted by the previous government.

Minerals and Mining Sector

The mineral industry started with the 1851 gold rush. Thousands of prospectors flocked from all over the world to the diggings. The small-time manual mining of that time contrasts with today's giant mechanised mining operations, although in gold mining at least, the fossickers still operate.

A steelworks at BHP Ltd, Australia's biggest mining company.

Modern Day Gold Fossicking

With the development of hand-held metal detectors that can detect gold nuggets up to two metres below ground level, individual prospecting is making a comeback. Given the right equipment, technique and location, it is possible to disappear into "the bush" for the weekend and emerge with several thousand dollars' worth of gold nuggets to which you hold legal title.

The easily-extracted gold was exhausted from the Victorian goldfields during the 1870s. Larger scale deep pit mining continued but the gold rush community of self-employed miners gradually dispersed. Though the Victorian goldfields were significant, the really big gold fields were discovered about 40 years later, near Kalgoorlie in Western Australia, 1,500 km to the west.

Gold was the metal that started the mining industry in Australia. Later, other minerals from Australia's abundant reserves were developed. In the 20th century, the Australian mining and mineral extraction expanded to include most minerals: coal, gold, iron, aluminium, copper, zinc, lead and nickel, the last being the foremost amongst them. Australia is a leader in the development of mining technology. Today, Australian companies are world leaders in the mining industry and are amongst the most efficient mining operations in the world.

Australian Mining Industry

While the biggest mining company in the world is the British-based company Rio Tinto, Australian companies are major players in most markets. Australia's biggest company, Broken Hill Proprietary, ranks as follows in some of its major markets:

Mineral	BHP Ranking	World's Largest
Iron Ore	Second	Rio Doce of Brazil
Copper	Second	Coldeco of Chile
Manganese Ore	Third	Samancor of South Africa
Black Coal	Seventh	Coal India
Raw Steel	Fourteenth	Nippon Steel
Oil Reserves	Eighteenth	Royal Dutch/Shell

Source: BHP Corporate Economics. *In Perspective: An Overview of BHP's Position in the World's Resources, Commercial and Financial Markets*. South Pacific Publishing, December 1996

Mining is, in some respects, Australia's national niche industry that has attained a critical mass where it can readily provide development capital from its own earnings. The industry is large and wealthy enough to develop its own technology and spin-off products—such as specialised slurry pumps—which are themselves world leaders in their particular technologies.

Large Australian mining companies are also significant overseas investors. Some of these companies, such as Mount Isa Mines (MIM) and North Broken Hill, obtain more than 50% of their profits from overseas operations.

Australian Companies Mining Overseas

MIM is one of Australia's biggest mining companies based domestically on a long established copper, lead and zinc mine at Mount Isa in north-west Queensland. The company is jointly developing the Alumbrera Copper Mine of Argentina with a Canadian mining company and the Argentinian Government. Early revenue from the project has exceeded that of its home-based mine at Mount Isa.

North Broken Hill is another Australian mining company whose overseas earnings from mining operations in Argentina, Sweden and Africa exceed its domestic earnings.

Rather less successful has been the purchase by Broken Hill Proprietary (BHP) of the US company Magma Copper for $3.2 billion. In this BHP has repeated the experience of many Australian companies venturing into the competitive US market. Forays into the United States by large Australian firms, which take over ailing companies have, in general, been costly failures.

Agricultural Sector

Soil conditions in Australia are generally poor, with deficiencies in phosphorous and nitrogen (though this can be overcome by using fertilisers). In addition, rainfall is low and irregular. The country has a range of climates, from the tropical north to the arid inland areas and the temperate coastal areas of the south. Northern Australia supports beef cattle and crops like sugar. Southern Australia favours sheep and cereals like wheat.

Foreign Investment in Agriculture

A drift of small property owners represents an opportunity for the establishment of commercial ventures in agriculture. There are no restrictions on foreigners investment in agriculture. In fact, some of the country's largest holdings are run by foreign operators.

Substantial Foreign-Owned Agricultural Holdings

Queensland and Northern Territory Pastoral Company is a beef cattle operation fully owned by BT Australia (a subsidiary of the New York-owned Bankers Trust). This company runs 160,000 cattle on 2.7 million hectares that cover 12 properties, making it one of the 10 largest agricultural industries in the country.

The second largest foreign pastoral company in Australia is owned by the Sultan of Brunei.

History of Agriculture

In the 19th century, European colonists pushing into the continent carved out tracts of land for farming. These people were called "squatters" as they occupied land to which they held no title. The foreign office in London disapproved of squatting mainly because it thought an awkward precedent might be set back home where agriculture was being revolutionised under the Enclosure Act, where peasants were disenfranchised, then forced to work in the factories created in the Industrial Revolution.

Local colonial administrators took a more sanguine view of the issue. While the local authorities made desultory attempts to get the squatters to pay for the land they had occupied, as requested by the foreign office in London, the squatters merely responded by pushing further inland and occupying yet more land. The government eventually capitulated, granting the squatters leasehold rights to graze the lands they had taken over.

Grazing leaseholds were handed down from one generation to the next. In the 20th century, the descendants of squatters assumed the more genteel title of "pastoralists" and adopted the role of the landed aristocrats of Australian society. Pastoralists became politically active and influential well beyond their numbers.

To this day, pastoralists are still in occupation of vast tracts of Crown land situated well inland. Farms closer to population centres mostly stand on freehold titles, bought under land sales conducted by the Crown in the 19th century.

Australian Stations

Australian stations are, by land area, some of the biggest farms in the world, operating vast tracts of marginal agricultural land. The largest holder in the country is S. Kidman and Company, the famous pastoral company owned by the Kidman, Ayres and Clover families. The total holdings, spread over a number of stations, are 11.7 million hectares (1.5% of the area of the entire country). Only slightly smaller is the Stanbroke Pastoral Company with 10.1 million hectares.

Wool was the country's most important export throughout much of the 20th century; its price reached record heights during the Korean War. Like what happened in the 19th century, the economy of the country once again rode "on a sheep's back". Until the late 1950s, agricultural exports accounted for more than 80% of the country's exports. This was the era that projected images of wealthy Australian graziers loading sheep into the Rolls Royce cars they used to herd the flocks around their vast sheep stations.

Agriculture of the Present Day

The agriculture sector of the Australian economy is efficient. The typical farmer is commercially astute, scientifically well-informed and has a good network with his contemporaries in the agricultural

Wool was Australia's most important export in the 19th century, a status which persists today.

community. An increasing number of farmers have connected to the Internet, through which they receive up-to-date information on a variety of topics such as the latest advances in agricultural science, commodity price updates and weather forecasts. A typical example of a situation faced by the modern commercially aware Australian farmer is whether or not to sell the immature crop on the futures market six months prior to harvesting.

However, farmers cannot control agricultural prices, which are set by the global forces of supply and demand. Farmers are price takers. Prices of agricultural commodities have fallen and this is the primary source of distress in the agricultural community. Over the years, the agricultural sector has run up extremely large debts to the banking sector.

This has borne down particularly on the smaller family holdings with limited resources. As a result, a steady stream of smaller holders, brought down by bankruptcy or financial fatigue, has departed from the industry. The size of farms has increased as smaller holdings are absorbed by larger ones, which are increasingly held by commercial operators rather than single families. The number of rural holdings in Australia has fallen from more than 200,000 in the 1960s to 110,000 in 1997.

Farms have been mechanising for decades and the trend is still continuing. Agricultural labour force has been in decline for many years while labour productivity has risen. In 1966, 9% of the total workforce was employed on the land. By 1990, this had fallen to 5%. Agricultural output rose by 120% in the same period

Australian farmers face the problems of farmers everywhere— falling prices, bad weather, pest infestation, soil erosion and heartless bankers. Arguably, the weather in Australia is more erratic than most places. Even in the best of seasons, farming conditions are marginal, particularly in the naturally arid inland areas where droughts may persist for years on end.

Agricultural Products and Prices

In the past 150 years, the long-term real price of agricultural commodities has fallen. The agricultural sector has survived through improved efficiency and yields. However, signs are now emerging that the long-term price fall of agricultural commodities could be reversing.

Global Consumption of Food

Economists estimate that the global consumption of food will double in the next 50 years whereas the amount of land brought under cultivation may not increase at all. While crop yields have increased more rapidly than demand for food over the last 50 years, the opinion of agricultural scientists is divided as to whether the rate of increase of yields can be maintained. Some economists believe that food shortages will contribute to an increase in the price of most agricultural commodities in the 21st century.

The Badgers Brook Vineyard in Yarra Valley, Victoria. Wine was one of Australia's top money-earning exports in 1996.

Agriculture in Australia has seen increasing diversity. While the major agricultural exports are still the traditional staples of wool, wheat and beef, opportunities for other products exist. For example, in 1996, wine was Australia's top money-earning export to the United Kingdom.

In addition to its proven markets, the agricultural sector has experimented with exotic new products. New products, however, are risky. Many of them are popular for a while, then lose their appeal—like most fads. Some Australian agricultural products that have enjoyed fleeting popularity in recent years include avocados, macadamia nuts, jojoba beans, angora goats, emus and ostriches.

Promoters of new agricultural products tend to be over-enthusiastic about their new commodity. Most of these new age agricultural products are introduced at fancy prices, which reflect an initial scarcity of the product being introduced. Like the Dutch tulip bulb bubble of the 17th century, experience shows that these prices tend to collapse as the market becomes saturated with eager (and often inexperienced) speculators as distinct from investors.

The fact that the seasons are reversed in Southern Hemisphere Australia (summer in December and winter in June) creates its own market opportunities for agricultural products. A major industry has emerged—air-freighting out-of-season cut flowers to Northern Hemisphere markets. Another major export is fruit supplied during winter and spring in the Northern Hemisphere.

Service Sector

The Australian Bureau of Statistics defines the service sector as the sum of all industries other than mining, agriculture and manufacturing. Service industries thus cover wholesale and retail, cafes and restaurants, transport and storage, communications, finance and insurance, property and business services, and cultural, recreational and personal services.

The service sector is the largest dollar component of the Australian economy (64%). It employs the largest number of people—72% of the workforce—and involves 64% of private sector businesses.

Wholesaling and Retailing

In 1996, the value of goods sold through wholesaling and retailing was $70 billion.[1] As in most countries, the wholesale and retail industries in Australia are a mixture of large and small businesses. There has been a major shift away from retail strip shopping to shopping malls. In fact, some of the richest business people in the country are shopping mall proprietors. In recent years, the relationship between shopping mall landlords and tenants has been under strain as labour laws are relaxed and shops are expected to stay open for more hours per day. A number of supermarkets now offer 24-hour shopping, seven days a week.

Mail order shopping has been around for a long time without making big inroads into shop retail. The latest derivative of mail order retailing is shopping on the Internet. However, while

Australians are enthusiastic users of the Internet, Internet retailing has so far made little impact on the Australian retail scene.

Construction
The value of the construction industry in 1996 was about $45 billion spread across three sectors—residential (houses and flats), commercial (offices, shops, hotels) and infrastructure (roads, bridges, water and sewerage)—in about equal proportions.

Property Investment

Residential Property Property, particularly residential home ownership, has been a preferred form of investment for Australians, who have one of the highest rates of home ownership in the world. Seventy percent of Australians own their own homes

Investment in property, which rose in value over a long period—at least at the rate of inflation—seemed a sure-fire method to preserve savings. In addition, the Australian taxation system allows *negative gearing*, under which a person can offset interest on property loans against their personal income tax provided the property is rented (that is to say, they do not live in it themselves!). Negative gearing encouraged people to put their savings into property, such as blocks of flats, at the expense of other forms of investment. Rates of return on rented property have historically averaged around 5% after expenses.

However, the 1990s—a period in which the stock exchange has risen consistently and inflation has been low—has witnessed some change in investment sentiment. Alternative investments have been seen to be more attractive than residential property. In any case, compulsory superannuation is satisfying the propensity to save—previously met by personal savings. These days, people are more inclined to live in rented accommodation, investing any spare cash in the stock exchange and other investment ventures.

Commercial Property There have been several spectacular commercial property developments by foreigners in Australia. One of the attractions to foreign property developers, particularly to investors from Singapore and Hong Kong, is the vast acreage of undeveloped land in Australia, much of it in easy reach of a major centre. Many tourist developments in Queensland are owned by Japanese developers.

> **The "Mini City" Project**
> The Hong Kong-based company, Far East Consortium International, a 100% foreign-owned business, has purchased a 1000-hectare estate at Wallan, 50 km north of Melbourne. The company intends to transform it into a "mini city" of 550 villas, 400 "ranches" and sporting facilities, including an 18-hole golf course. The development is 30 minutes from Melbourne's main international airport at Tullamarine and about 45 minutes from Melbourne's CBD.
>
> Source: "Sunday Age", 5 November 1997

Tourism

In the Australian economy, the industry that has grown most rapidly in recent years is tourism, which contributed 68% of service sector export earnings in 1996. Consultancy and education are the service sector's other main export earning industries.

During the 1950s and 1960s, the service sector had a large import imbalance. However, recent years have seen a remarkable increase in inbound tourism. With the growth of income and cost of living overseas, coupled with cheaper airfares, Australia has become an inexpensive international destination. From 1991 to 1996, Australian tourism (in dollar value) rose at an average annual rate of 15.6% and the number of visitors rose by an annual rate of 11.9%. By comparison, the number of Australian tourists travelling overseas increased at 5.4% per annum for the same period.

Tourism is now a net export industry, with overseas tourists in Australia out-spending Australian tourists abroad.

Tourism contributed 7% to GDP in 1996, of which around 75% was attributable to domestic tourism. Tourism is thus an important industry to the national and regional economies, and one which federal and state governments actively promote.

The tourist infrastructure has improved greatly with the development of more facilities and additional attractions. In the period 1997–1999, approximately $1 billion per year is expected to be spent on additional hotel and motel accommodation nationwide. Tourism is also expected to receive additional impetus from the 2000 Olympic Games in Sydney.

The largest increases in tourist numbers have been from nearby Asian countries, in particular Japan.

Country of Origin of Overseas Visitors—1996

Country	Number of Visitors	Percentage
Japan	813,000	19.5
New Zealand	671,000	16.1
South East Asia	648,000	15.6
Other North East Asia	596,000	14.3
Other Europe	410,000	9.9
UK & Ireland	388,000	9.3
USA	316,000	7.6
Rest of the World	319,000	7.7
Total	4,161,000	100

Source: Office of National Tourism, DIST BR 025/96

Processed Food

Australia has adopted multiculturalism as an official policy. Each immigrant group is encouraged to maintain its customs, including food. Australian diet is truly cosmopolitan: it has no identifiable single origin. White Anglo-Saxons, the predominant ethnic group, consume indiscriminately across the entire range of imported diets. Furthermore, a wide range of foodstuffs is always available as Australia is a vast agricultural nation with many regional climates.

The diversity of foodstuffs available in Australia has expanded greatly since the 1950s. At the same time, consumer preference has shifted from the standard meal of red meat and three vegetables to include fish, poultry, pasta and vegetarian dishes as well. Restaurants offering the food of all national diets are popular among Australians of all ethnicity. There is a ready market in Australia for imported specialist foodstuffs, and plenty of scope for those who wish to establish food vending businesses serving their own national dishes.

Information Technology and Communications

As in the rest of the world, information technology and communications is one of the fastest growing sectors of the economy. The information technology market in Australia was worth $14.5 billion in 1995, and is projected to reach $19.9 billion by 1999.

Until 30 June 1997, there were two major competing telecommunications corporations in Australia—Telstra and Optus—providing cable networks that cover almost the entire country. However, under new government regulations, the number of telephone companies operating in the country is unrestricted as of 1 July 1997.

State and federal governments have taken a particularly pro-active role in developing the information technology and communications sector. A number of quasi-government bodies have been founded to promote communications technology, such as the Collaborative Information Technology Research Institute (CITRI), the Australian Artificial Intelligence Institute (AAII), and the Australian Computing and Communications Institute (ACCI).

Many of the world's major computing and communications suppliers have operations in Australia.

Secure Network Solutions

The are many parts to the information technology industry. Opportunities exist for large and small firms. For example, the Australian company, Secure Network Solutions, which employs about 40 people, recently developed a data security system under a consultancy agreement with a retail bank. The product, similar to a credit card, combines a modem and ISDN connection to encrypt and scramble the data prior to data transmission. The estimated worth of the 1997 global data security market is US$6.3 billion and it is expected to double by the year 2000.

The Australian communications industry generated revenues of $26.7 billion in 1995, of which $20.2 billion were revenues of carriers. The balance was revenue derived from communications equipment. The Bureau of Industry Economics forecasts sales of computing and communications equipment to grow at about 10% per annum through to 2005.

Education

Business opportunities in the education sector are available in higher education services, particularly those in association with other countries.

As English is the international language of commerce, English language courses—for Asians, in particular—are a profitable line of business.

In 1997, the credit card company, MasterCard, conducted an education survey in 13 Asia-Pacific countries. It found that the percentage of MasterCard holders who intended to send their children overseas for an education was 57% in China, 46% in Hong Kong, 35% in Thailand and India, 33% in Japan, and 31%

in Singapore and Taiwan. In contrast, the country least likely to educate its children overseas was Australia—8%.

A net benefit of the English-speaking education boom will flow to Australia, provided that Australian educational institutions become involved. Inevitably, Australia is in competition with other English-speaking countries in this market. The MasterCard survey found that the country of first choice for English-speaking overseas education was the United States (43%), followed by the United Kingdom (21%) and Australia (20%). Australia's perceived advantages were the cheaper cost of courses and accommodation, and the proximity of the country to the students' home country.

In 1996, Australia had about 1% of the world market for overseas students—estimated at US$100 billion. Australian education exports in 1996 were A$2.3 billion (approximately US$1.7 billion). Most of this amount is for courses conducted in Australia. Provision of Australian education service overseas, usually in coordination with overseas educational institutions, represents $100 million of the sector earnings. The major scope for expansion is in the Asia-Pacific region.

With the rising popularity of the Internet, courses by correspondence may develop quickly. Opportunities also exist in the development of innovative programmes in telecommunications and distance learning.

Banking

In the wholesale market, banks are permitted to operate as overseas-owned operations. However, banks that want to operate in the retail market must be incorporated locally. Retail banking in Australia is dominated by four locally-owned banks—the "Big Four"[2], which have a very strong position in the domestic market. They have extensive overseas operations as well.

After the financial markets were de-regulated in 1984, several foreign banks started operations in Australia. Though there are some restrictions on foreign ownership, the banking industry offers opportunities for foreign entrants, due largely to negative sentiment in the community regarding the current crop of major banks.

The larger banks are not popular in the community, which sees bankers as remote and exploitative. All four of the big banks are running cost-reduction programmes, closing unprofitable branches in poverty stricken rural towns and firing staff across the board—tarnishing the image of banking in the community. The banks plead the need to remain competitive, but the public image of the Big Four banks is exacerbated by wide media coverage of record banking profit announcements and the astronomical salaries of banking executives.

Big Salaries for Your Local Banker

The salary packages of Westpac Banking Corporation allow executives the option of buying company shares on favourable terms if the share price goes up. The CEO of Westpac since 1992, Robert Joss, was by mid-1997 showing a paper profit of $25 million on his share options—in addition to his salary and other benefits. Eight hundred and nineteen executives of the bank were also cut into the deal, showing aggregate paper profits on non-salary benefits of $164 million among them .

Across the street at the National Bank of Australia (NAB), the CEO Don Argus was making more modest progress, having accumulated $7.7 million paper profits on his NAB share options in approximately the same period.

Source: *The Age,* 28 June 1997

The atmosphere of "big bank bashing" helps create a commercial environment where the smaller banks find it easier to succeed than they otherwise would. A number of smaller regional banks, such as St. George's Bank, Challenge Bank and Bank of Melbourne, have taken advantage of this sentiment and have won disaffected customers from major banks, promoting in particular, the idea of more personalised customer service. Retail banking is therefore open to new entrants running smaller operations with a more sympathetic public image.

Recent History of Banking The stock market crash of 1987 prompted the collapse of several banks and financial institutions.

Past Governments and Banking
Caught up in the entrepreneurial excesses of the 1980s, the Labor governments of Victoria and South Australia decided to convert their cautious but profitable state-owned retail banks into merchant banks. Both appointed new CEOs to guide their banks in this new direction.

However, the state banks of Victoria and South Australia, which had both operated profitably for over 100 years, rapidly ran into bankruptcy under their new CEOs and were taken over by other banks.

Other financial corporations were also victims of the crash. The government-run commercial lending institution, the Victorian Economic Development Corporation, failed and was wound up. The Pyramid Building Society also collapsed, with lenders bailed out by the Victorian State Government. Similarly, the Estate Mortgage Building Society failed and depositors lost their money.

The aftermath of the stock market crash of 1987 left banks with non-performing loans which had to be written off balance sheets of the late 1980s and early 1990s. However, as computerisation lowered costs and unprofitable branches were closed, banks were able to rebuild their balance sheets. By the mid-1990s, the banking sector had fully recovered from the crash of the 1980s. The biggest bank in the country, the National Bank of Australia, was Australia's most profitable company in 1996. While all of the "Big Four" have become involved in banking operations overseas by taking over regional banks in other countries, opinion is divided in local banking circles whether any of the "Big Four" is, itself, a takeover target by an overseas bank.

Efficiency and Profitability of the Banking Sector The difference between interest paid to depositors and interest charged to lenders—known as *spreads*—have generally been higher in Australia than in most countries. This makes banking in Australia a highly profitable activity. The Big Four banks have sometimes been accused of colluding in setting interests rates. However, investigations undertaken by the Australian Competition and Consumer Commission (ACCC) in response to such accusations have always exonerated the banks and found that the competitive marketplace is working properly.

According to a McKinsey & Co. survey, retail banks in Australia performed poorly, relative to international best practice, despite attempts by banks to increase efficiency through measures such as encouraging customers to transfer funds electronically.

The Fully Automated Bank

Studies by banks have shown that the cost of electronic banking is only 10% and the cost of ATM transactions is about 25% of the cost of manual banking. However, consumer resistance to electronic fund transfer has required that banks keep manual operations going. Banks are cautious about moving into the electronic age quicker than their customers can adjust. In 1996, a bank in the United States, which adopted 100% electronic banking, lost all its customers and was wound up.

Staff salaries represent about 60% of total costs in the banking industry. Therefore, the motivation for banks to cut down on staff is high. The National Australia Bank is putting the fully-automated branch on trial at twelve locations. Such a branch would have no staff at all, conducting all banking operations—including the issue of housing loans—through an interactive terminal.

In addition, the government imposes some social obligations on the major banks, such as the requirement to maintain uneconomic branches and the provision of *deeming accounts*[3] for pensioners. These obligations reduce the overall profitability of the banking system. In recent years, competition from specialist finance providers has increased, particularly in home loans.

Other Financial Institutions

In addition to banks, a wide variety of other financial institutions such as finance companies and credit unions also exist in Australia. As in the United States, non-bank finance providers in the finance industry are minimally regulated. Prudential supervision is conducted by several institutions—the Reserve Bank of Australia (RBA), the Australian Securities Commission (ASC) and various other regulators under the umbrella of the Australian Financial Institutions Commission (AFIC).

In the United States, non-bank finance providers have more than half of the home loan market. The proportion is far less in Australia, suggesting potential for growth. The non-bank area of the financial services market has grown in recent years and represents an on-going opportunity for new entrants.

Monetary Investment in Australia

Both state and federal governments market government fixed interest bonds domestically and overseas. These bonds are backed by government guarantees and are virtually risk-free. Government-owned statutory corporations also raise money this way. As a general rule, bonds of statutory corporations are also guaranteed by the issuing government. Various banks and commercial institutions issue a wide range of fixed interest securities.

Opportunities for Government Business

Since the late 1970s, federal and state governments have adopted increasingly laissez faire principles by selling public corporations to the private sector. Major public utilities, such as power and gas companies, have already been sold or are in the process of being sold to private enterprise. Most of the successful bidders for utilities sold in the 1990s have been foreign-owned companies.

In addition to utilities, some sections of the railways and the post office are likely to be privatised as part of the government's desire to divest itself of commercial corporate activities.

In addition to the outright sale of public corporations, the contracting out of government services to private corporations represents another major opportunity for foreign business. Both the state and federal governments are in the process of downsizing their bureaucracies by contracting out services that were previously provided by direct-hire staff. Generally speaking, foreign-owned businesses are not restricted from tendering for these activities. In some cases, where an objective in the specification of the contract is to adopt some specialist overseas-owned technology, foreign bidders may even be preferred.

Information regarding such business opportunities is widely available. Future tender opportunities are advertised in newspapers and can also be obtained from the Internet.

CHAPTER 3

The Australian Government

Overview—Government in Australia

There are three layers of government in Australia—the federal government, state government and local government. A foreign business person is likely to deal with each layer. Business people visiting the country need to understand how Australia's administrative turf is split amongst the various bureaucracies.

Under the Australian federal system, the state, federal and local governments struggle ceaselessly to maintain and increase their powers, even when the same party is in office at both the state and federal levels.

Overlaying the normal checks and balances of a healthy democracy are conflicts between one branch of government and another. Whichever party is in power, the House of Representatives (the lower house) is in permanent conflict with the Senate (the upper house) since the Senate is permanently controlled by independents. The federal government is also in conflict with the state governments—who squabble amongst themselves, mainly for a larger share of public funds. The Australian political system operates as a series of feuding fiefdoms. Under this political system, the pursuit of cogent national policies is virtually impossible.

Added to this are the short electoral periods (three years for the federal government and some states and four years for others) and the fact that none of the state elections coincides with each other or with the federal election. At any one time, an election is likely to occur somewhere in the country. Since the federal government is always sensitive to its party prospects in the states, the country is almost permanently in election mode.

Summoning the political will or the political courage to tackle the hard issues has been beyond all the administrations of the last

20 years. Under the present political structure (which can only be changed by referendum), the country is unlikely to produce a leader with the stature and authority of, for example, Singapore's Lee Kuan Yew. There are simply too many political schisms in Australia for such a leader to realise his or her vision.

Australian Political History

Australia's three-layered political structure is the consequence of British settlement. New South Wales was the first Australian colony. This was followed in the early 19th century by separate penal colonies declared in Tasmania (1825), Western Australia (1829) and Queensland (1859). Free settlers, rather than convicts, founded the colonies of South Australia (1834) and Victoria (1851).

During the 19th century, each of the Australian colonies was administered separately from London. The colonies had little contact with one another. However, as the country developed, interaction between the colonies increased.

Towards the end of the 19th century, the political will for Australia to federate into a single country developed in the colonies and London. The new nation was formed at the dawn of the 20th century and declared in Britain under the Commonwealth of Australia Act. On 1 January 1900, the colonies of New South Wales, Victoria, Tasmania, West Australia, South Australia and Queensland (now called "states") united into a single country called the Commonwealth of Australia.

The document that enshrined the rules for this new country was called the constitution, and those who wrote the constitution became known by the respectful term—the Founding Fathers.

One of the first tasks of the Founding Fathers was to locate the seat of the federal government. Neither of the two biggest population centres, Sydney or Melbourne, was suitable as the two cities had already joined a rivalry that has continued to this day. Neither could concede the mantle of national capital to the other.

The compromise site chosen was Canberra, approximately half way between the Melbourne and Sydney. While Canberra is entirely within New South Wales, the area around Canberra was declared an independent territory—the Australian Capital Territory (ACT)—so that neither of the two main states of New South Wales and Victoria would be favoured.

Women in Parliament

No "Founding Mothers" were in politics at the turn of the century to contribute to the constitution. In 1903, Vida Goldstein stood for the federal Senate—the first female candidate to offer herself for election in any government in the British empire. At the time, women had the vote in only two states of the Commonwealth. Vida Goldstein was unsuccessful.

The first female politician to win a seat in federal parliament was Edith Lyons (later Dame Edith Lyons) representing Darwin in Tasmania on behalf of the United Party (since renamed the Liberal Party). Dame Edith, who was elected in August 1943 to the House of Representatives, started with a political advantage. She was the wife of Joe Lyons, the prime minister of Australia from 1932 to 1939.

The Constitution

The purpose of the constitution was to define which powers were to be retained by the states and which were to be passed on to the federal government to be administered on behalf of the newly-formed nation. Historically, the constitution was an agreement between colonialists who did not entirely trust each other. As drafted, the constitution enshrines vested interests as they were at the time of federation.

The constitution broadly established that matters of a national character like customs, defence and immigration should be undertaken by the federal government while matters of a more local nature were undertaken by the states. Areas like health and education overlapped, with the Ministries of Education and Health (with attendant bureaucracies) at both state and federal levels.

Since federation, there has been some drift of state powers to the Commonwealth. However, a major preoccupation of state parliamentarians has been to protect their turf. Transfer of state powers to the Commonwealth has proceeded at glacial speed.

Changes to the split of responsibility between the state and federal governments require constitutional amendments, which themselves can be passed only by referendum. Subsequently, for a referendum to be constitutionally acceptable, it must be passed by a two-thirds majority of votes in every state—an outcome that has rarely been achieved.

While safeguards of the constitution have succeeded in preserving its integrity, they have also hampered political progress. In practice, only in the rare cases where the subject of the referendum received the unanimous support of all political parties, have the referendum proposals been approved. As a result, the constitution has become progressively more outdated.

Constitutional Amendments
Since the time of federation, 42 proposals for referendum have been put forward, of which only eight have been carried out—resulting in 24 constitutional amendments. The last successful referendum proposal was in 1975.

Government Hierarchy

Federal Government
The federal government, sitting in Canberra, comprises an upper and lower house based on the Westminster model. The lower house, called the House of Representatives, initiates bills in the same way as the House of Commons in Britain. The upper house,

The Parliament House in Canberra is situated in the Australian Capital Territory and is an independent territory 482 km from Sydney.

called the Senate, is the house of review. Presiding over the entire apparatus of government is the governor-general, an individual appointed by the British Crown. For most of the 20th century, people thought that the office of governor-general was a purely ceremonial position. However, this notion was shattered in 1975, when the then governor-general, Sir John Kerr, succeeded in dissolving the Labor government of Gough Whitlam.

Seats to the House of Representatives are distributed in proportion to population. However, the constitutional basis of the Senate is different. Each state sends 12 representatives to the Senate so that every state, large or small, speaks with an equal voice. Senators are elected en bloc for each state rather than by individual electorates, which tends to entrench minority parties and independents. The 1984 legislation to increase the size of the Senate from 60 to 72 members exacerbated this problem. The enlarged Senate enabled parties like the Greens to hold the balance of power in the country with as little as 8% of the primary vote.

Controlled by minorities, the Senate frustrates or modifies government legislation, rendering whichever party in power at the federal level a perpetually lame duck administration.

Telstra

To get the Senate to pass its controversial proposal to sell a third of the telephone company Telstra, the 1997 federal government had to engage in a "pork barrelling" exercise with two independent senators, one from Tasmania and the other from Queensland. This resulted in the expenditure of $600 million to support the pet projects in the electorates of the independents.

State Government

The state governments also retain the trappings of their colonial origins. Each state has a separate constitution and a state governor appointed by the British Crown, each occupying a separate Government House within each state capital city—just the way it was in the colonial days of the 19th century. State governments (with the exception of Queensland) have two upper and lower houses based on the Westminster model. The names of houses vary among states. The lower house is typically called the Legislative Assembly and the upper house, the Legislative Council.

While the leader of the country holds the office of prime minister, the state leaders are called premiers. Both state and federal governments come with the full retinue of ministries and bureaucratic assistance. The prime minister and premiers form cabinets (seven cabinets for the whole country, all acting independently) with both federal and state ministers appointed to portfolios—some of them covering the same function at both the state and federal levels. Both state and federal ministers have departments of public servants working for them (seven sets of separate bureaucracies working under seven different sets of rules).

In addition to the states, there are the Northern Territory and the Australian Capital Territory, which have most of the characteristics of states and their own bureaucracies.

Local Government
The third tier of government is the local councils that look after municipality affairs such as local roads, garbage collection and local infrastructure. Councils are run by councillors elected by the ratepayers of the municipality. They operate under the Local Government Acts of the various states.

Electoral System
Australian elections use a *preferential* voting system to determine the outcome of elections. This method of vote-counting is worth mentioning for its curious value and its effect of producing surprising election results, which further weaken the power of majority parties.

The Preferential Voting System
Under the preferential system, voters must rank their preference from first to last—from the candidate they like the most to the candidate they like the least. Each candidate must be ranked for the vote to be valid. The winner is determined when one candidate has a clear majority (more than half the total number of votes) rather than a simple majority (more votes than anyone else). In elections involving more than two candidates, to achieve this clear majority, "preferences are distributed". One of the odd effects of distributing preferences is that a vote ranking a candidate second last on one voter's ticket may, after preferences are distributed, count equally with a vote where the candidate was ranked first. Almost no one in the community understands this consequence of the preferential voting system.

Another peculiarity of Australian elections is that voting is compulsory. Whereas in less democratic societies, jails are crammed with agitators denied the right to vote, Australian prisons have contained at least one citizen who was jailed for demanding the right *not* to vote. In Australia, voters who fail to cast their votes at any of the country's frequent elections are fined.

The ABCs of Australia's Voting System

In 1996, a Melbourne citizen, Albert Langer, paid the ultimate penalty for not voting (claiming that none of the candidates was worth voting for). He went to jail for 10 days after he failed to pay a $10 fine for not voting in the federal election of that year.

Others with no political interest attend the polling booth on election day merely to avoid a fine. Once there, they are given a voting slip, on which the candidates are listed in alphabetical order of surname but not identified by party. A significant percentage of the total electorate (estimated as high as 5%) then vote "straight down the list", thereby favouring candidates whose surnames are closest to the front of the alphabet. This, the so-called donkey vote, has encouraged parties to select candidates whose surnames start with an early letter of the alphabet!

Parties in Government

There are currently three main political parties in Australia, the Liberal Party, the Labor Party and the National Party. These parties exist at both federal and state levels. Though the policy distinctions between the parties have become blurred in recent times, broadly, the Liberal Party is right-wing, the Labor Party is left-wing and the National Party represents the agricultural community.

The Liberal Party and the National Party are natural allies and have successfully joined forces to form the federal and state governments several times since World War II. This arrangement is called the coalition. Generally, either the Labor Party or the coalition will hold a majority in the House of Representatives over the combined forces of the opposition party, plus the few seats held by independents.

When the coalition is in power federally, the leader of the Liberal Party becomes the prime minister and the leader of the National Party becomes the deputy prime minister. Similarly, when the coalition is in power in a state, the leader of the state Liberal Party normally becomes the premier and the leader of the state National Party becomes the deputy premier.

The only significant minority party is the Democrats, which sees its role to be—as the party's founder Don Chipp was fond of saying—"To keep the bastards honest" (the "bastards" being whichever of the two major parties is in power and holding the majority in the House of Representatives). The Democrats have never succeeded in winning a seat in the House of Representatives but have, since 1980, held the balance of power in the Senate, either by themselves or in combination with independents.

Operation of Government

With its three layers of government, each person in Australia is represented by five politicians—one representative each for the upper and lower federal houses, one representative each for the upper and lower state houses, and one councillor in local government. The number of politicians in Australia—sum of federal and state, not counting local councillors—is 839 or one per 21,500 of the population, which is one of the highest rates of political representation anywhere in the world. The total number of councillors in the country is around 10,000.

With the gradual transfer of administrative powers to the Commonwealth, the responsibilities of the states has been reduced over the years and the time spent conducting state affairs has diminished commensurately.

The states are at a financial disadvantage with respect to the Commonwealth because they lack sufficient tax-raising powers

Victoria's Upper House
In 1996, 44 parliamentarians from the Legislative Council of Victoria—Victoria's upper house—sat for a total of 26 days and 15% of the legislative councillors made no contribution to the government during that year. In addition, a number of legislative councillors had the time to undertake full-time jobs in the private sector to supplement their $150,000-a-year parliamentarian salary/benefits package.

to fund all their operations. Funding in excess of that raised by state taxes is allocated by the Commonwealth. Every year, the state premiers gather in Canberra to attend the usually acrimonious meeting, the Premiers' Conference, to receive their funding allocations from the federal treasurer.

Corruption
A 1995 New York Times survey based on the perception of business executives and journalists found that perceived corruption in Australia was similar to that of its main trading partners.

Corruption Index

Country	Corruption Index
New Zealand	9.55
Australia	8.80
United Kingdom	8.57
Germany	8.14
United States	7.70
Japan	6.79
Indonesia	1.94

* The higher the corruption index, the lower the corruption

Recently, state governments and their attendant bureaucracies have been more corrupt than their federal counterparts. The main area of corruption has been in the awarding of contracts for state government services without a proper tendering procedure. It may well be that for foreign companies contemplating bidding for such contract work, fostering the right political connections may be more beneficial than quoting the best product at the lowest price.

The aftermath of the 1987 stock exchange crash exposed scandals involving state governments in Australia. In particular, the Labor government of Western Australia had become embroiled in an unholy alliance with some fairly dodgy businessmen who were riding a crest of entrepreneurialism in the state at the time.[1]

Government, Business and Corruption

Western Australia's premier in 1987, Brian Burke, used funds belonging to the State Government Insurance Commission (SGIC) to bail out *nouveau riche* multimillionaires whom the crash was threatening to reconstitute as ordinary mortals.

To bail out Australia's then richest individual, Holmes a Court, taxpayers of Western Australia bought $500 million of his property and share assets through the SGIC. To bail out the merchant bank Rothwells owned by Laurie Connell, who owned 400 racehorses, the state provided a $150 million taxpayer-funded loan guarantee. To bail out the biggest entrepreneur of them all, Alan Bond, the state bought his diamond mines at fancy prices.

Connell, Bond and Burke all subsequently went to jail for various offences, and Holmes a Court died from a heart attack.

In the same period, in Queensland, the National Party government was involved in business dealings that ultimately saw its premier, Sir Joh Bjelke Peterson, taken to court on corruption charges. Sir Joh had, for years, run a government that appeared to favour "mates" as his close associates were known. After the evidence was heard at Sir Joh's trial, the jury could not agree on a verdict. The charges against Sir Joh were unproven and Sir Joh was acquitted. Soon after the trial, the press published the story that the jury's foreman, whose insistence of Sir Joh's innocence had been unshakeable, was an office holder of the National Party.

After the heady days of the late 1980s, entrepreneurialism in Australian business subsided. Commerce reverted to corporatists. An altogether duller period ensued, much less prone to corruption, during which share prices gradually recovered.

By the mid-1990s, most of the governments of the late 1980s had been replaced by governments of the opposite political persuasion. By this time, the privatisation, outsourcing and bureaucratic downsizing of government services were in full swing. Federal and state governments called tenders for the activities being privatised—a process that presented new opportunities for state government corruption to surface.

Corruption in the Government

The Liberal government in Victoria's contracting out of services has been criticised by the state's auditor-general to be excessively secretive and possibly corrupt The auditor-general pointed out that the successful contractor for the construction and operation of the Melbourne Casino won the licence despite not being the highest bidder. Furthermore, one of the major shareholders of the successful bidder was the treasurer of the Liberal Party of Victoria and a personal friend of the Victorian premier.

To rebut the auditor-general's criticism, the Victorian state government then appointed a committee of three—one of whom was a director of the successful Casino bidder—to investigate the auditor-general!

Inevitably, the committee's recommendation was that the auditor-general's audit powers be curbed. As its auditor-general, the state wanted a lapdog, not a watchdog.

At the petty bureaucratic level, Australia has little corruption. Bank notes need not be tucked into your passport when presenting it for visa applications and any attempt to bribe a traffic officer would probably be unsuccessful and may bring further charges.

Dealing with Bureaucracy

In its endeavours to improve the country's trade performance, the government exhorts industry to adopt the "world's best practice" by using the latest technology, adopting the most efficient work practices and trying to qualify for the ISO 9000 series of standards.

As its own contribution to "world's best practice", the government has undertaken to deliver *microeconomic reforms* to the country. This all-embracing term includes providing a better physical infrastructure and imposing less bureaucracy.

The government recognises that dealing with the bureaucracy is a significant business cost. With the objective of reducing bureaucracy, all three levels of government are cooperating to create a single point of contact for enquiries regarding all aspects of the public sector. The objective is that by the year 2001, activities of the government and public utilities may be obtained from a single Internet enquiry.

Directory of Government Departments

A single directory to all state and federal government departments, titled *National Guide to Government*, has been produced by a commercial firm, Information Australia.

Rules Relating to Foreign Investment

While Australia generally encourages foreign investment, a few restrictions apply.

The law relating to the acquisition of Australian domestic assets by foreigners is the Foreign Acquisitions and Takeovers Act of 1975.

One of the provisions under this act is that the purchase of real estate requires the approval of the Foreign Investment Review Board (FIRB). Purchase of an existing residential dwelling will normally not be approved unless the dwelling is for occupancy by an employee of a foreign corporation established in Australia. On the other hand, real estate proposals to buy land for building development will normally be approved.

Foreign ownership is also restricted in industries such as the media and in the major Australian trading banks.

Foreign Ownership

Foreigners can acquire Australian-owned assets, such as existing companies, without approval if the investment is less than A$5 million.

Foreign control of Australian-owned assets greater than A$5 million is not prohibited but requires FIRB approval.

Under the Foreign Acquisitions and Takeovers Act, *foreign control* is defined as ownership by a single foreign individual or corporation of greater than 15% of the voting shares in the company owning the assets, or the aggregate ownership by foreign owners of greater than 40% of the voting shares.

Should the investment proposal require approval under the act, foreign investors should not be dissuaded from applying to the FIRB. Historically, except for the purchase of developed residential property, FIRB approval is granted in 98% of cases.

The foreign ownership rules are subject to frequent change. To assess the eligibility of an investment scheme, a local accounting firm should be contacted for the latest guidelines.

Other Investment Rules

The federal government aims to maintain a competitive marketplace trading in an ethical manner. The Trade Practices Act imposes rules to restrict takeovers that concentrate the market against public interest. The Trade Practices Act also prohibits dubious or dishonest trading practices such as misleading advertising, price tampering, pyramid selling and the sale of dangerous or illegal goods.

The federal watchdog for ensuring compliance with the Trade Practices Act and other fair trading legislation is the Australian Competition and Consumer Commission (ACCC).

Government Programmes to Assist Business

Firms undertaking innovation and product development can apply for the relief of corporate income tax. Approved R&D projects can be written off at 125% of actual costs incurred.

The R&D Start programme, run by AusIndustry (the commercial arm of the Department of Industry, Science and Tourism), is a scheme that provides funding to Small and Medium Sized Enterprises (SMEs) for approved research projects. The Australian Industry Development Corporation (AIDC) sponsors approved business start-ups as a lender, shareholder or both. However, funding under both the R&D Start and the AIDC is available only to Australian-controlled companies, in which the foreign investor can have at best, only a minority interest.

As was seen during the government's Tariff Review of 1997, industry lobby groups can materially affect the government's policy settings—even those comprising foreign companies.

The Productivity Commission

In 1997, the government's Productivity Commission was commissioned to advise the government on the recommended level of tariffs for the car industry for the ensuing 15 years.

The Productivity Commission recommended that tariffs on imported cars be cut progressively from 22.5% to 5% by 2004.

The government wanted to implement this recommendation but had its mind changed by a car industry lobby group comprising representatives from the four car manufacturers in Australia—General Motors, Ford, Toyota and Mitsubishi—all of which are 100% foreign-owned companies.

Whether formal programmes of assistance exist, state and federal governments may be prepared to offer all sorts of concessions and benefits to tempt a particular project into their sphere of influence.

In 1996, the federal government's Productivity Commission made a study of the total amount spent by all states offering incentives for businesses to locate in their particular state.

The Productivity Commission estimated that the aggregate annual public money expended on such incentives was $2.5 billion in direct support and $4.8 billion in foregone payroll tax—figures that are greater than the entire amount collected in tariffs for the whole economy ($3.8 billion).

The Bega Cheese Cooperative

In 1997, the New South Wales Labor government beat the ACT in a bidding war for a cheese cooperative to locate its 150-job project in its state. The NSW Government lent the Bega Cooperative Society $20 million to establish the cheese cooperative and provided an additional $800,000 subsidy to the society for a staff training programme.

Enticements offered by state governments to persuade businesses to locate in their state include favourable deals on purchase or lease of land, easy loans, payroll tax exemption and exemptions from normal planning permissions, such as environmental regulations—even straight-out cash.

Motives for offering incentives vary from government to government and from deal to deal. It is generally based on some form of political rivalry between the states. This rivalry is felt not only at the government level but also at the individual level—by the person in the street who feels a tribal attachment to their state or city. Sometimes, the opportunity arises for an enterprise to exploit the parochial feelings of citizens for commercial advantage.

The Australian Grand Prix

From 1985 to 1995, the annual Australian Formula One Grand Prix was held in Adelaide, the capital of South Australia. These races were generally popular with the people of Adelaide although they almost always ran at a financial loss.

In 1992, the Liberal Party attained control in Victoria, replacing the Labor Party during whose term of office, a number of financial mishaps had dented the confidence of the state. A policy of the new Liberal government was to restore the Victorians' sense of pride in their state and thereby secure their future votes.

A representative acting for the state government was sent to London to convince Bernie Ecclestone—the British entrepreneur who owned F1 Promotions, the company that runs Formula 1 racing worldwide—to change the location of the Australian F1 Grand Prix from Adelaide to Melbourne.

The amount of Victorian taxpayers' money paid to persuade Ecclestone to grant this favour has never been revealed, although $25 million is the popularly reported figure. Under a policy termed Commercial Confidentiality, the Victorian Government conceals from taxpayers almost all details of its monetary dealings with the business sector. Another $100 million of taxpayers' money was spent building a new racetrack.

Each year, the Melbourne Grand Prix makes a financial loss, yet the majority of Melbournians are in favour of it. Not only does staging the Grand Prix ignite a sense of Melbournian pride, but winning the event from Adelaide was also a poke in the eye for the "Croweaters"—as the South Australian rivals from across the western border are disparagingly termed.

Partly as a result of the Grand Prix and other "feel-good" measures taken on behalf of the electors (and at their expense), Victorians rewarded the Liberal government with a landslide victory in the 1996 election. Curiously the $50 per head paid by Victorian taxpayers to secure the event that they so emphatically wanted to stage did not even buy them a ticket to see it.

As a footnote, by the end of 1996, Ecclestone's net worth was reported to be $87 million, having doubled in the two years that he had business dealings with the Victorian Government.

Prices Surveillance Authority

The general thrust of government policy has been to allow market forces to control prices. However, in the markets for essential goods serviced by only a handful of suppliers, the government has appointed a prices watchdog to protect consumers. This body, the Prices Surveillance Authority (PSA), has the power to conduct price enquiries and make recommendations to the government.

Tax

Tax reform in Australia has been a controversial issue for a number of years. For a long time, most economists have agreed that the existing tax system is over-weighted towards the taxing of economic inputs, such as income and payroll, and insufficiently weighted to tax consumption. Forty-three percent of Australia's tax take is raised as personal income tax, whereas the existing wholesale sales tax raises only 8%. Economists have, for many years, proposed the introduction of a new tax—the goods and services tax (GST)—and the scrapping of the existing sales tax, which is easy to evade.

The tax reform proposed is not revolutionary and is nothing more than the value added tax (VAT) regimes that most countries (with the notable exception of the United States) have had for years. In fact, Australia and the United States are the only OECD countries not to have VAT. However, attempts to introduce GST into Australia have been met by voter resistance and misinformation campaigns by political opponents.

Federal Taxes

Tax in Australia is raised by all three tiers of the government. The federal government collects the lion's share of the total tax harvest, including personal income tax, corporate income tax, sales tax, fringe benefit tax, capital gains tax, customs and excise duty, and various other forms of taxes like taxes on petrol, alcohol and

Proposed Goods and Services Tax (GST)

The GST has been proposed and opposed many times. In 1985, when the federal Labor Party was in power, the treasurer Paul Keating proposed to the cabinet that GST be adopted under his so-called Option C plan. Prime Minister Bob Hawke, who was not noted for his strong political will, rejected the idea on the grounds that it would be difficult to sell to the electorate and in particular, to the trade unions.

In 1993, the Labor Party was still in power but was expected to lose the coming election. The Liberal Party bravely proposed GST as part of their election platform. The same Keating who, eight years before, had personally recommended the tax to his then leader, won the 1993 election by scaremongering enough of the electorate into believing GST was a tax increase rather than a tax redistribution.

As a consequence in the 1996 election, the Liberal Party (under the command of John Howard—another leader not noted for his political will) was gun-shy about the much needed tax reform and deferred the issue to yet another electoral period in the future.

However, there does appear to have been a change in sentiment in the community, with the majority now favouring the tax. If this sentiment persists, political parties will no doubt adjust their policies accordingly. A fairly well-established Australian political principle states that "where the people lead, the leaders will eventually follow".

cigarettes. So far, the tax gatherers of Australia have not levied taxes like death duty, wealth tax and inheritance tax found in some other countries.

Personal Income Tax (43% of the total tax take)   Everyone who works in Australia must obtain a personal *tax file number* that uniquely identifies them as an income-earning taxpaying individual (if they do not obtain a tax file number, taxation charged on their earnings is punitive).

Companies employing staff must also obtain another number called the *group number* from the Australian Tax Office (ATO), obliging employers to collect income tax from the wages and salaries of their employees.

Income tax collected from employees is remitted to the ATO monthly or once in three months by the employer. At the end of each financial year, the employer provides each employee of the company with a statement of earnings and taxes paid—the *group certificate*—with which employees file their tax returns.

At the end of the financial year, the employer also provides the ATO with one copy of the group certificates of all employees, together with a reconciliation of payments to prove that the employer has remitted to the ATO all taxes deducted from the wages of employees.

Australia is party to reciprocal taxation agreements with most countries. A foreigner earning a salary in Australia is liable to Australian income tax only on income derived in Australia. Whether tax is payable on interest and dividends earned in Australia varies with the situation.

The income tax laws in Australia are now so complicated and subject to such frequent change that most Australians engage a tax agent to prepare their tax returns. Foreigners earning income in Australia are advised to do the same.

Fees for the preparation of tax returns depend on the degree of complication but usually start at about $80 per return (for individuals as distinct from corporations) and are themselves an eligible tax deduction.

Company Income Tax (13% of total taxation)   Income tax is payable on the company's annual profits after the deduction of all expenses, excluding dividends on shares. The company income tax rate varies occasionally but has remained at 36% for a number of years.

Australia attempts to avoid the transfer of profits made by companies from Australian trading operations to offshore tax havens. Australia is a signatory to taxation treaties that seek to combat tax avoidance by tax minimising transfer pricing schemes. Under this legislation, the deduction allowable for the cost of goods purchased from a closely associated company, such as another branch of an overseas-owned corporation trading in a third party country, is limited to the real value of the goods being transferred. Tax treaties are intended to keep the profits made in Australia properly subjected to Australian tax, thereby protecting the Australian tax base.

Intercompany transactions between local companies are also subject to transfer pricing rules designed to reduce corporate income tax.

Federal Excise Duty (10.9% of total taxation)   Excise duty is levied by both the state and federal governments on goods such as petrol, alcoholic beverages and tobacco products. Excise duty is collected by the vendors of the products concerned and included in the retail price of the goods.

Sales Tax (8% of total taxation)   Sales tax is charged on some sales transactions while others are exempted from it. It is assessed by applying a percentage to the wholesale price of the goods. The sales tax applied varies with the nature of the goods, and the rights and entitlements of the buyer. Some goods are exempt from sales tax, for instance, fire safety equipment and some foodstuffs.

Buyers such as government departments, invalids holding doctors' certificates and companies holding sales tax exemption certificates are also exempt.

One of the main problems of the tax is that the amount of taxation levied depends on the category under which the goods are described. This produces an endless supply of absurdities for critics of the system to illustrate their points.

The Vagaries of Sales Tax

It has been mischievously suggested by a prominent advocate of tax reform[2] that a recent apparent trend in Australia of weddings without formal engagements is due to the different categories of sales tax allocated to engagement rings and wedding rings. An engagement ring attracts 22% sales tax whereas no sales tax is levied on wedding rings.

Other examples of the vagaries of sales tax assessment are:

- Staple foods such as biscuits may include sales tax whereas the luxury food, caviar, does not.
- *Strawberry Quik Drink* and *Chocolate Quik Drink* differ only in their flavouring. However, *Strawberry Quik Drink* includes a sales tax whereas *Chocolate Quik Drink* does not.

In addition to the difficulty of correctly categorising the goods, the sales tax presents another complication. Unlike other consumption taxes such as VAT and GST levied in other countries, the sales tax is not incurred by the value-added transactions in the production chain but at the single point where the goods are sold by a wholesaler to a retailer or end user.

Determining the point in the production distribution chain at which tax is levied (called the *taxing point*) determines the amount of tax paid since the lower the notional price of the goods, the lower the tax incurred. Although sales between wholesalers and retailers are meant to be "at arm's length", some manufacturing companies find it worthwhile to set up separate retailing companies so that they can first sell the goods to themselves at an artificially low "wholesale price" before on-selling the goods to customers through their retailing arm. In this way, the notional wholesale price and therefore, sales tax levied, is reduced.

Investors setting up a manufacturing operation should note that they will be entitled to sales tax exemption on raw materials only if they obtain a sales tax exemption certificate. To obtain sales tax exemption, the manufacturer applies to the Australian Taxation Office for a sales tax exemption number. When obtained, the sales tax exemption number is displayed on the company's purchase orders.

Sales tax sounds simple. However, for those involved in manufacturing, it may not be. The Sales Tax Act has become a tangled maze of regulations and amendments. The principal sales tax problems are to define what transactions are exempt, to categorise goods and to define the taxing point.

Manufacturers setting up operations in Australia are advised to consult specialist sales tax consultants who can recommend the right corporate structure to set up to minimise sales tax obligations and in particular, establish the taxing point. Sales tax consultants, who make a living from resolving the complications of sales tax issues, are usually ex-employees of the Australian Taxation Office.

For goods that are ordered internationally over the Internet, sales tax will be assessed by the Customs Department and paid for by the consumer on collection of the goods, along with the excise duty, if applicable.

If GST is eventually introduced, the sales tax will be abolished and these elaborate processes will (at least theoretically) no longer be necessary.

Customs Duty (3.8% of total taxation)   Tariffs are levied on certain goods imported into Australia. Similar to sales tax, the rate of customs duty will vary with the nature of the goods being imported. Anyone importing goods into Australia is advised to appoint a customs agent to take care of all aspects of importing, including the (very complex) paperwork for the assessment of duty. Customs duty must be paid to the Department of Customs prior to the goods being cleared for entry into the country. Alternatively, the goods may be held in a "bonded warehouse" operated by Australian Customs. If stored in a bonded warehouse, customs duty must be paid upon collection of the goods.

Fringe Benefits Tax (1.1% of total taxation)   Fringe benefits tax was introduced in 1986 to draw into the tax net hitherto untaxed earnings or non-cash benefits such as company cars, accommodation assistance, children's school fees and medical costs.

A calculation of the fringe benefits tax can take considerable administrative effort as the definition of 'benefits' is far-reaching. For example, even the provision of a car parking space at work is considered a fringe benefit. Fringe benefits tax regulations change frequently—typically once a year at budget time (which is the month of May in Australia). A tax accountant should be consulted for the latest updates.

Capital Gains Tax (0.3% of total taxation)   Capital gains tax was introduced[3] on 19 September 1995. It applies to the capital gains on assets bought from that day. In assessing the tax, the capital gain is indexed for the consumer price index (CPI). The amount of the capital gain for the year is then added to the income for the year and taxed at the marginal income tax rate.

Capital gains are only incurred when the asset is sold and the capital gain is realised. Capital losses may be offset against capital gains but only if they are both incurred in the same year. Tax planning at the end of the financial year thus requires that gains and losses be balanced—with the object of ensuring that tax deductibility of capital losses is fully realised. Liability for capital gains tax is incurred by nonresidents of Australia only on the portion of income earned in Australia.

State Taxes

The state government collects payroll tax, stamp duties, financial institutions duty and land tax. The level of taxes varies from one state to another. The most highly-taxed state is Victoria, the state which has traditionally been Australia's industrial heartland.

State Excise States impose additional excise (the level of which varies from one state to another) on most of the goods that already attract federal excise duties. These include petrol, alcoholic beverages and tobacco products.

Stamp Duty These taxes are incurred as transaction taxes when assets are bought and sold, or when leases for future transfers of benefits (such as rental agreements) are signed. Stamp duty is a percentage of the value of the transaction. The levy varies from one state to another, and from one type of asset to another.

Payroll Tax These taxes are levied on gross wages at a rate that varies from state to state. The average rate of taxation is about 7%, with about the first $500,000 of the payroll being tax-exempt.

Financial Institutions Duty and Bank Accounts Debits Tax The mere act of effecting a financial transaction will attract two taxes. The financial institutions duty (FID) is levied on amounts received into accounts while the bank accounts debits tax (BAD) is levied on amounts debited to accounts. These taxes are collected by the financial institution involved in the transaction (usually a bank) which remits them to the taxing authority. The rate of tax varies from state to state and depends on the size of the transaction attracting the tax. The account holder will first see these taxes as deductions on bank or financial statements.

Royalties and Resource Rent Tax

Federal and state governments collect royalties from mining ventures. The rate at which the tax is collected varies with the state, the mineral under consideration and even between one mineral extraction facility and the next (each of which may be subject to a different royalty agreement). For investors contemplating delving into the mining industry, tax details can be obtained from a tax accountant.

Dividend Imputation

In 1986, the federal government amended the tax laws to avoid double taxation of share dividend income. The objective was to increase the attractiveness of equity investment. Hitherto, dividends on shares had effectively been taxed twice—firstly, on the company profits that generated the dividends and secondly, as personal income. The scheme to relieve this double taxation burden was called *dividend imputation.*

Under dividend imputation, share dividends derived from after-tax profits are termed *franked* and carry with them *franking credits* that can be set against other income.

Share dividend income is thus taxed once, at a rate determined by the overall income position of the shareholder. From a foreign investor's viewpoint, the principal question is how the franking credit can best be used—a consideration that requires specific accounting advice to suit the particular situation.

The Australian Government does not restrict the importation or repatriation of capital or the repatriation of dividends.

Corporate Tax Strategies

There are different types of corporate entities available as the vehicles for foreign investment operate under different tax regimes. The objective for investors will be to minimise the aggregate taxes incurred by the enterprise within Australia and overseas. The optimum strategy will depend on the respective tax regimes prevailing in Australia and the investor's country of origin. To establish the most tax-effective arrangements, investors proposing to establish an enterprise in Australia should seek tax advice at an early stage and certainly before incorporating their business. The tax effects of transfer payments, dividend repatriation, franking credits and the legitimate home office costs that can be passed through to Australian operations will vary, depending on circumstances. A local accounting firm can be sought for advice.

Failure to Pay the Required Tax

Companies or individuals who fail to collect or pay the stipulated taxes may be heavily punished by the Australian Tax Office (ATO), with penalties up to 200% of the underpaid tax being levied by the ATO at its discretion. While avenues of appeal, including the legal system, are available through which objections to tax rulings perceived to be unfair can be made, any penalties imposed by ATO must be paid pending the outcome of objections.

International Comparison—Taxation Levels in Australia

Tax reform is a fertile subject in Australia that arguably generates more debate than action.

Investors can note that, compared to other countries in the OECD, Australia is not a highly taxed country. In 1994, the total tax take in Australia was 29.4% of GDP compared to the OECD average of 39.4%. While the collection of taxes is a little complicated, in particular the sales tax, the government has succeeded in simplifying tax administration in recent years.

For each type of tax payable—group tax, sales tax, payroll tax, etc.—the federal or state government responsible issues a separate booklet containing clear guidelines for assessment of the tax. In addition, virtually all accounting software written in Australia will automatically compute the tax payable and issue reminders to users when tax payments are due.

A business in the formative stages will customarily engage a tax accountant to structure the specific business in a way that tax will be minimised. Administration of taxes throughout the business year is generally within the capability of a competent bookkeeper.

The Financial Year

Situated in the Southern Hemisphere, the seasons in Australia are the reverse of the Northern Hemisphere. Summer starts on 1 December and winter on 1 June. Australian business pretty much goes on a holiday the week before Christmas, from which it fully emerges only about the third or fourth week in January. In this period, operations like car assembly plants or chemical plants do their annual maintenance or plant modifications.

As most of your staff will be absent, the end of the calendar year would therefore be the worst possible time to end the financial year and balance the books. To reflect this reality, the financial year has been set halfway through the calendar year. It runs from 1 July to 30 June of the following year. Virtually all commercial operations within the country, including the taxation system, operate to this timetable.

CHAPTER 4

Infrastructure, Science and the Environment

Overview

Australia has well-developed transportation and communications systems to support business enterprises undertaken in the country. Its scientific institutions are world-class. However, the country faces environmental problems, some of which are peculiar to its own unique ecosystem while others are shared with the rest of the world. Addressing environmental issues opens markets for new products and presents great opportunities for the business sector.

Infrastructure

Unlike countries in Europe and Asia where earlier societies left vast structures such as the Egyptian Pyramids and the Great Wall of China, the indigenous inhabitants of Australia built virtually no permanent physical structures at all. Up till the time of European settlement, anything the Aborigines made—shelter and weapons—was from timber and other biologically degradable materials. Except for some cave paintings, the 50,000-year Aboriginal occupation of the continent has left few tangible remains. The entire physical infrastructure of the nation has been built in the 200 years of European settlement.

A present day map of the Australian rail and road systems reflects the history of infrastructure development. On the mainland of Australia, there were five major settlements where the five present capital cities are located. Each state capital is a centre for the road and rail systems. The 19th century transport systems spread out from the cities and met at state boundaries.

The rail system left from colonial days has proven impossible to integrate because the colonialists of the 19th century constructed their railway systems using three different gauge tracks spread over five states. What seemed like a good idea at the time—to build railway systems of different gauges to reduce competition—has left the federated country with an enduring nightmare of incompatible rail tracks and rolling stock.

Transport

National Highways and Interstate Road Transportation The road system in Australia is the responsibility of all three layers of government. The federal government looks after the network of interstate highways. The state governments are responsible for secondary highways and freeways within cities, and the major roads traversing municipalities. Local councils look after suburban streets.

On heavily travelled routes such as those between Sydney and Melbourne, highways are mostly freeway standard dual carriageways which bypass most of the towns along the way. Most of the road system connects populated areas around the coast. In the outback and over in the west, roads are fewer. The north-south Stuart Highway cuts through the interior of the country and connects Darwin and Adelaide, while the east-west Eyre Highway connects Western Australia to the rest of the country.

Given the country's low population density, the road system is of a good standard (though some Australians may disagree). However, much of the secondary road network is still unsealed gravel. Circumnavigating the country by road, a distance of about 12,000 km, is still an adventure that few Australians have accomplished. Off the main highways and in the interior, one finds dirt tracks, sometimes poorly marked and maintained, suitable only for experienced drivers travelling in convoys of four-wheel-drive vehicles. Even today, inexperienced travellers are occasionally stranded by mechanical failure in a hot, unforgiving and featureless country, where death by dehydration may be only hours away.

Australian traffic drives on the left side of the road. Standards of road construction, signage, permissible axle loads, bridge load limits, permissible speed limits and even rules of the road can vary somewhat between states. The contiguous countries of continental Europe have succeeded in standardising their road rules and signage better than the six states of Australia.

The bulk of the country's freight travels by road. Semi-trailers ply routes all over Australia. In the more remote regions, *road trains* with double and triple articulated trailer trucks (respectively called *B-doubles* and *C-triples*) are widely used.

A large number of privately-owned freight companies operate trucks, from owner-drivers to trans-national corporations. Since road freighting is a highly competitive market, freight rates are not excessive despite the distances travelled.

Airways International airports offering immigration facilities and customs services exist at all state capital cities, Canberra and Cairns—a major tourist destination in Northern Queensland.

Sydney's Mascot Airport is the country's busiest and Melbourne's Tullamarine Airport handles the most freight.

Air traffic into Sydney is such that inbound flights are frequently delayed. Airport extensions to Mascot have been proposed to alleviate the congestion. The airport is located in a developed area and local residents have so far successfully resisted all proposals to extend the airport and, in particular, to build a third runway. An endless number of hearings are conducted in regard to the location of a second airport.

Most interstate business travel within Australia is by air. Two competing airlines, Qantas Airways and Ansett Airways, operate air services between major cities. Smaller airlines or private charter planes serve subsidiary routes. From time to time, third airlines— mostly unsuccessful—have been started up to compete with Qantas and Ansett. The few third airlines that survived have eventually been taken over by one of the major carriers.

Though the majority of freight travels by road, an extensive air cargo system handles urgent deliveries. All interstate mail travels by air. In recent years, the average annual rise in the volume of air travel within Australia has been 7%.

Railways Generally, rail transportation—other than for commuter travel within cities—is not as developed in Australia as it is in, for example, the European countries. The development of rail transport within Australia has been hampered by the different rail gauges between the various states.

Australian Rail Gauges

The rail gauge for New South Wales and South Australia is 4' 8 1/2" (1435 mm), which is the same as Europe and the United States. In Australia, this is referred to as the *standard gauge*.

The gauge in Queensland, Western Australia and Tasmania is 3' 6" (1067 mm), and in Victoria, it is 5'4" (1626 mm).

Standard gauge lines now connect most of the capital cities but there are no plans to standardise the gauges of local or provincial networks within the various states.

Railways are mostly state-run operations although Australian mining companies have built private rail systems to transport bulk mineral ores from inland mines to the coast for shipment overseas in bulk ore carriers. Since the 1960s, standard gauge tracks—such as that between Sydney and Melbourne, and the Indian Pacific Railway across the Nullarbor Plain from Sydney to Perth—have been laid into the states with nonstandard gauge tracks.

Freight services on the standard track lines are operated by the National Rail Corporation (NRC), which is owned by a

The Flinders Street railway station in Melbourne, the heart of the Melbourne commuter system.

consortium of federal and state governments. NRC operates a number of innovative long-distance freight operations by rail, including the *Bi-modal* freight. Here, the entire trailing portion of a container road semi-trailer is moved by rail on the "long haul" between Perth and Melbourne, and transported via the road system at each end of the journey. NRC commands about one-third of the interstate freight business.

As commercial entities, publicly-owned rail freight companies have broken even or made profits in recent years. However, passenger trains have long been loss-making operations subsidised by the state. Nevertheless, some passenger railways have already been privatised and further privatisation is likely in the future.

West Coast Railway
The first privatised passenger rail service was the West Coast Railway, which serves provincial routes in Western Victoria. Under privatisation arrangements, the state continues to be responsible for track maintenance while West Coast Railway operates the rolling stock to an acceptable level of service.

Shipping   All the capital cities, including Darwin have international shipping facilities such as container unloading. In addition, there are a number of international and regional ports mostly dedicated to shipping specific bulk primary products such as coal, iron ore, wheat and live sheep. An important part of the government's agenda for microeconomic reform is the upgrading of facilities and the improvement of work practices on the docks, with the twin objectives of increasing efficiency and reducing costs. In 1996, container clearance rates and shipping costs to Pacific destinations were a little higher than the average for other international ports.

In addition to international shipping facilities, a limited amount of coastal shipping exists, mostly restricted to bulk cargoes such as coal and iron ore. Goods between the mainland of Australia and the island state of Tasmania are freighted by ship.

Imcat
One of Tasmania's most successful business ventures, Imcat, manufactures aluminium catamarans for use as ferries. Although Imcat mainly exports to the European market, it has introduced the 6000 tonne cargo-carrying catamarans on the Bass Strait route between Tasmania and the Australian mainland. The wave piercing 80 m long catamarans are four times as fast as conventional ships, thereby radically improving Tasmania's accessibility.

There is a fairly strong movement by the governments to contract out services within the ports, even to the extent of privatising the entire ports. For example, the Port of Geelong and the Port of Portland in Victoria have both been privatised and are entirely run by private operators.

Australia has its own federal government-owned shipping line, the Australian National Line (ANL), which it has attempted to privatise—so far without success. This line is strongly unionised and employs only Australian labour working under Australian labour conditions. ANL is thought to have uncompetitive costs when compared to other shipping lines flying flags of convenience.

Long Distance Bus Services A network of long distance bus services connects all the capital cities and major provincial towns in Australia. Two-thirds of the country can be circumnavigated by air-conditioned coach. There are extensive holiday routes into places like Alice Springs in the centre of the country.

Around the City Cars can be hired at most airports and can usually be booked ahead on the plane. Taxis are readily available everywhere and always work on metered fares. Public transport varies from one city to the next and can be a combination of trains and buses. Melbourne has the world's most extensive electric-powered street tramcar network.

Utilities

Electricity Historically, government-owned public corporations were developed to supply power in each of the states. Over the years, physical boundaries between state utilities have blurred. Today, power generators in the various states sell power across state borders in increasing quantities. A National Grid has begun but is not yet fully developed.

Since the early 1990s, the privatisation of government-owned power utilities has gathered pace. The power networks are vast enterprises and the privatisation strategy has been to split them up into separate entities based on geographical area and function.

For the purposes of privatisation, the power network has been broadly split into power generation companies, power transmission companies and power distribution companies.

Privatisation programmes are run separately in each state by the government of that state. The majority of successful bidders for power companies under privatisation programmes have been foreign-owned utility companies, each sold as separate lots.

A benefit of privatisation to the consumer is the ability to negotiate with different utility companies for the supply of power. Competing power companies will enter individual tariff structure negotiations with large power consumers. Since privatisation, some reports claim reductions in the cost of power of up to 40%. Smaller consumers have a weaker bargaining position.

Like railways, power supply utilities developed independently in the various states. Unlike railways, electrical standards are uniform throughout the country. Voltage at point of use is 240 v 50 Hz single phase or 415 v 50 Hz three phase. For large installations, 6,000 volts or more can be acquired on negotiation. Quality of power is of world standard. Most of the power comes from coal-fired generators. Supplementary base load hydro power is produced by the Snowy Mountain Irrigation Scheme in New South Wales and also in Tasmania. In some states, gas-fired generators supply peak load requirements.

Despite possessing the world's largest reserves of uranium, Australia has no nuclear reactors generating electricity and no commercial nuclear reactor programme. Public sentiment is against nuclear power generation. In fact, the Australian Government cannot find a place in any part of the whole vast continent to bury spent fuel rods from its one scientific nuclear reactor at Lucas Heights outside Sydney.

Despite this antipathy to the products of the nuclear industry, the community is sanguine about the mining of uranium ores, of which Australia has the world's largest reserves and is the world's second largest supplier.

With its abundant sunshine and vast distances, Australia would seem a natural venue for alternative power generation methods such as solar power, wind power and tidal power. A couple of the country's premier scientific research institutions could reasonably claim world leadership in solar technology. However, the development of alternative power has attracted only limited interest in the government.

The state governments of Western Australia, South Australia and Queensland run small schemes for solar energy development. However, the 1996 Liberal federal government scrapped the Energy Research and Development Corporation Programme established by its predecessors with the aim of developing alternative energy sources.

Coal is the primary source of power in Australia. Liberal Party policy on power generation and greenhouse gas emission is greatly swayed by the coal mining lobby which wants to use all the coal it can. The mining industry is an important financial supporter of the Liberal Party.

Oil and Gas   Australia has several small oil fields but the country is a net importer of oil. Natural gas was introduced to domestic consumers in the 1960s, with the development of gas fields in the interior of the country and the Bass Strait—the stretch of sea between mainland Australia and Tasmania. Vast gas fields have also been developed off the north-west coastline of the country, where the gas is liquefied and shipped to Japan. All state capital cities and most provincial towns have piped gas. Failing that, bottled gas is available for domestic and commercial consumers.

Water Supply and Sewerage   Piped water and piped sewage disposal are available to all but the smallest of communities. Water supply and sewage disposal are generally handled by the same authority—either a local council or a more broadly-based regional authority. In recent years, some of the water supply and sewage disposal authorities have been privatised, often by foreign companies. For example, in 1995, a single contract was written with a British-French consortium to operate the water supply and sewage disposal systems of Adelaide. The future will present further opportunities for commercial entities interested in these activities.

Solid and Liquid Waste Removal   There are severe penalties in all Australian states for the illicit dumping of waste—particularly toxic, hazardous or non-biodegradable liquid waste. Effluent standards vary according to the particular jurisdictions but are fairly strict by international standards. An entire industry exists in the country for the collection and disposal of both liquid and solid waste. Waste must be classified by toxicity and biodegradability, according to guidelines that can be obtained from the Department of the Environment of the particular state in which the business is located. The approved method of handling the waste depends upon its classification.

Communications

Telecommunications   In Australia, telecommunications is one of the fastest growing areas of the economy—as it is in the rest of the world. In a country of vast distances and low population, the development of telecommunications in Australia was an early political imperative. The result is that Australia has built itself a comprehensive telecommunications network over the years. For many years, the publicly-owned telephone company, Telstra (previously known as Telecom), was Australia's largest and most profitable commercial institution. In recent years, a competitive telephone company, Optus Communications, was formed and in 1997, the privatisation of Telstra itself began with the proposal to sell one-third of its shareholding.

New telecommunications technology has readily been adopted by Australia. The country has one of the highest coverage of mobile phones in the world (exceeded only by the Scandinavian countries). The network includes the access to international circuits for voice, data and broadband users, and the recently "rolled out" domestic cable network for cable TV and connection to the information system.

Telecommunications within Australia and between Australia and the rest of the world is reliable and cheap by world standards.

Internet   A recent innovation is trade through the Internet where, in its ultimate expression, the entire sales transaction can be conducted electronically—from the specification of the goods, to its purchase, delivery and payment. The Australian federal government's endorsement of Internet trading was granted at the Internet Trading Forum (ITF), launched by the Minister for Trade, Tim Fischer, in Perth on 2 May 1997.

The ITF is a joint initiative between Trade Match International (TMIL) and the Confederation of Asia-Pacific Chambers of Commerce and Industry (CACCI), with the object of facilitating contact between buyers and sellers. The ITF is an Internet marketplace open to buyers and sellers in which data is matched from within the ITF database or from the Trade Match CD-ROM database. As Internet use grows, its use as a sales medium is likely to increase rapidly.

The Post Office   Australia was the first country in the world to introduce prepaid mail. The practice, which originated in New South Wales in 1838, preceded the introduction of postage stamps in Britain by two years. The Australian postal system is run by a federal government-owned corporation Australia Post, whose motto is "We Deliver". For the most part, they do.

The postal service is cheap, reliable and efficient, with a 95% percent next-day-delivery rate within metropolitan areas. The cost of post is 45 cents for a standard weight letter delivered anywhere in Australia. All interstate letter deliveries are by air. A variety of mail services are offered including *Express Post*, which guarantees 24-hour mail to any place in the country. Post boxes offering the advantages of anonymity, security and convenience are readily available on application to Australia Post.

Postal delivery is an industry under competition from an increasing number of alternative systems. Over the years, the means of sending messages has moved from telex to fax and most recently, to e-mail. According to an Australia Post survey, the number of messages delivered within Australia by electronic mail (fax and e-mail) exceeded ordinary mail for the first time in 1997.

There is fierce competition in Australia for delivery services for packages and parcels. In major cities, many types of parcel delivery companies (one of which is run by Australia Post) offer pick-up services from your doorstep and deliver directly to your customer at prices from $5 per package. On longer haul freight, Australia Post competes with the highly competitive private road freight companies.

Despite the competition from technology and alternative delivery systems, Australia Post operates profitably, having cut costs and diversified into areas like the supply of stationery and computer products. In 1996, Australia Post declared a profit of $240 million, of which $142 million was remitted to the government as a dividend. All or part of Australia Post is slated for future privatisation and therefore, presents a business opportunity for companies specialising in courier and mail services.

The Sydney Harbour Bridge in Australia's largest industrial city.

Brief Description of the Infrastructure in Each State

New South Wales (1996 population: 6.1 million)   NSW is Australia's most populous state. Its capital city, Sydney, is the largest city in Australia with a population of 3.8 million. Sydney is located in a fabulous geographic setting of rugged ocean coastline and extensive inland waterways. Large secondary cities in NSW include Wollongong and Newcastle.

The head offices of most banks, and finance and insurance companies are located in Sydney, which is also a major centre of the manufacturing industry. The Wollongong area south of Sydney is the site for BHP's biggest steelworks. NSW is the nation's most important agricultural producer and the principal beneficiary of the Murray Darling irrigation system. Although Sydney is Australia's most expensive city, 80% of North American companies select Sydney as their headquarters to serve the Pacific Rim region.

Victoria (1996 population: 4.5 million) This is Australia's second most populous state. Although Victoria is the smallest of the mainland states by area, its capital city, Melbourne, is the second largest city in Australia with a population of 3.2 million. Large secondary cities include Geelong, Ballarat and Bendigo.

Melbourne is the home of the car industry (GM, Ford and Toyota) and heavy industry such as petrochemical and plastics. Melbourne has worked hard to banish a reputation for blandness, jazzing up its image by attracting glitzy sporting events and glamour industries. In this vein, Victoria is the only known government in the world to have appointed a Minister of Multimedia. Victoria produces a full range of temperate agricultural commodities and has interesting tourist attractions.

Queensland (1996 population: 3.3 million)   Queensland is Australia's most decentralised state with 1.5 million people or 50% of the state population living in the capital city of Brisbane. Major provincial cities include Townsville, Cairns and Rockhampton, with Australia's premier tourist attraction, the Great Barrier Reef, running parallel to the Queensland coastline. Surfers Paradise near Brisbane is the country's most popular tourist centre.

Queensland has the fastest growing population of all Australian states, with people moving in from the southern states, particularly from Victoria. The climate is tropical or semitropical. Queensland has extensive mining and extraction industries based on coal, aluminium, gold, copper, lead and zinc. It is also an important agricultural producer of animal products and crops, including sugar.

Western Australia (1996 population: 1.73 million)   Western Australia is Australia's biggest state by geographical area. The capital city is Perth, a lovely, clean city with a population of 1.3 million. Much of the state is desert or semi-desert, with the fertile parts in the south-west and north-west corners. The climate ranges from temperate to hot-dry desert conditions.

Western Australia is Australia's biggest producer of gold, iron ore, nickel and liquefied natural gas. The south-west of the state is an important producer of wheat and forest products. The north-west supports extensive cattle stations.

South Australia (1996 population: 1.45 million)   The capital city is Adelaide, a very attractive city that has a population of 1.1 million. South Australia has a dry climate and is largely desert or semi-desert.

The Borossa Valley in the Adelaide Hills is Australia's biggest wine growing district. Crops such as wheat are grown in the eastern part of the state and on the Eyre Peninsula. A major mining project is the copper and uranium Olympic Dam project in the interior of the state. Adelaide is a major centre for the car industry.

During the 1980s and 1990s, the industrial and population growth rates in South Australia have been lower than the surrounding states. This has led the South Australian Government to offer incentives for industries to locate in the state and to devise creative projects such as the Multi-function Polis to attract industry.

Tasmania (1996 population: 470,000)   Tasmania's capital city, Hobart, has a population of 195,000. Hobart is attractively situated on the estuary of the Derwent River and the slopes of Mount Wellington. Tasmania is the smallest of the states, with an economy based on agriculture and mineral products from mining operations in the western part of the state.

Northern Territory (1996 population: 174,000)   Its capital city is Darwin, which has a population of 81,000. The Northern Territory economy is based on agriculture, mining and tourism. The Kakadu National Park is a major tourist attraction for both domestic and international travellers.

Australian Capital Territory (1996 population: 304,000)   The ACT is the seat of the federal capital, Canberra. It is the headquarters for many of the federal departments. The economy of the ACT is based on the business of government. Canberra is a pleasant open city, built from a master plan drawn up at the turn of the century.

Science

Over the years, Australia has produced a number of outstanding scientists over a broad range of disciplines, particularly medicine. Australians have won many Nobel prizes.

Australian culture values creativity and curiosity. The country has been one of the fastest to embrace new technologies such as personal computers, mobile phones, ATMs and the Internet.

At the individual level, most Australians have a "can do" attitude to technology that may sometimes exceed their real abilities. The cultural roots of this engaging trait are probably historical. Early settlers pushing into the hostile interior developed their wide ranging skills merely to survive. The attitudes to "have a go" (sometimes at projects that are beyond them) and "no worries" (optimism that the project will turn out right in the end) are part of the Australian psyche.

Australians are strongly individualistic and less group-orientated than the people of some other cultures. "Doing it yourself" rather than obtaining assistance from an expert is a practice many Australians like to adopt. By and large, Australians are not daunted by tasks like renovating their homes (a national pastime), doing a spot of plumbing or electrical wiring or fixing their cars. In the Australian workforce, these attitudes can be both useful and dangerous.

Scientific Institutions in Australia

The premier scientific research body in Australia is the Commonwealth Scientific and Industrial Research Organisation

(CSIRO), a fully government-owned institution of world repute. The CSIRO undertakes both fundamental and applied science on its own account and in partnership with commercial companies.

For investors interested in developing technologically-advanced projects within the country, the CSIRO—a truly outstanding institute of science and technology—can assist in a variety of ways, including consultancy services, collaborative research and development agreements, and technology licence agreements. The specialist fields for which these services are available include food production and processing, telecommunications and electronics, agribusiness, and prototyping. For a full list of services provided, the CSIRO website can be accessed on the Internet.

The State of Science

Scientists and engineers are poorly paid in Australia and have low status, which contrasts oddly with their achievements, abilities and high academic standards. In government, commerce and the community at large, the level of scientific comprehension is low. The difficulties of pursuing a career in science in Australia have prompted the exodus of some of the best scientists (the "Brain Drain") to countries where science and technology are more highly paid and better appreciated.

Many Australians have a larrikin inventive streak and produce truly ingenious products. The rate of commercial development is low, however, as Australian commercial institutions are very risk averse and product development funding is hard to get.

Australia is, therefore, a good hunting ground for people who have ideas but lack the means to develop them. An astute foreign investor has the opportunity to buy up rights or patents cheaply and develop them either within Australia or overseas.

Australian non-scientists tend to have a negative image of their own country's scientific ability. Australian big business and government are dominated by lawyers and accountants who are

---

Australian Inventions Developed Overseas

Some Australian inventions, which found no domestic backing, have been developed commercially overseas. These include the black box flight recorder, over the horizon radar and the Sarich orbital engine. Products successfully developed within the country range from the pop top can to the atomic absorption spectrometer.

One of the most exciting prospects currently is the nano-machine, which is a biosensor one hundred thousandth of a millimetre in size, with moving parts the size of individual molecules. Developed by the CSIRO and commercial interest groups, the machine has the potential to transform agriculture and medicine as it has the ability to identify gene sequences and detect the minutest quantities of organic material

---

mostly anti-science—particularly Australian science. There are no scientists at all in the Australian Government and very few engineers. No Australian Government has ever appointed a Minister of Science who was a scientist.

Every now and then, a government comes along that says it thinks differently. The government of Bob Hawke (prime minister from 1983 to 1991) sought to reduce the country's balance of payments problem by encouraging manufactured exports. Hawke coined the phrase "The Clever Country" to describe what he hoped Australia might become if it could direct its scientific and technological talents towards a worthwhile economic objective. The idea was to encourage Australia to become an innovative country, creating ingenious products for export to the world.

In 1985, the government introduced tax incentives to stimulate the manufacturing industry to innovate and thereby develop new exportable or import-replacing products. Principal amongst these was a 150% tax deduction for expenses incurred on approved research and development projects. Whether as a result of these measures, or for other reasons, research and development increased during the years, 1985 to 1996.

Towards the mid-1990s, creative accountants managed to find ways to frustrate the objectives of the 150% R&D tax deduction programme. A minor industry was established, advising unethical firms on ways to exploit loopholes in the legislation and claiming the R&D tax break without undertaking the R&D itself. In the Australian vernacular, the nefarious activity of plundering the public purse carries the label, *rorting*.

In 1996, with the twin objectives of shutting down the R&D tax *rort* and reducing the budget deficit inherited from the outgoing Labor government, the incoming Liberal government reduced the tax incentive for R&D to 125%. At the same time, it implemented a new package of direct R&D incentives.

Studies by the Australian Bureau of Statistics have shown that R&D is much more likely to be conducted by small high-tech companies employing less than 200 people and run by technologically-competent managers or owners. These findings motivated the government to introduce a programme of financial assistance called R&D Start to encourage innovation by small to medium-sized enterprises (SMEs) with a genuine interest in R&D. The programme provides financial assistance to help develop new product ideas which involve a high technical risk.

The size of projects covered under the scheme is about $10 million or less. The programme is coordinated by AusIndustry, a subsidiary of the Department of Industry, Science and Tourism. Only technically-competent local firms with a turnover of less than $50 million are eligible for this scheme. While primarily directed at local industry, firms with equity shared between local and foreign shareholders may be eligible.

Multi-function Polis

In an effort to encourage high-tech industry to its region, the state of South Australia is subsidising the development of a Multi-function Polis (MFP) within the environs of Adelaide.

The objective of the MFP is to create a technology-based "Smart City" with 3,700 houses in an area equipped with special cabling for computers, security, site-wide broadband, Local Area Network (LAN) computing, video conferencing, high-speed data and mobile IT services, and advanced integrated education facilities linking businesses, universities and the community. The philosophy of the project is that high-tech industries will be encouraged to establish themselves in "Smart City" by virtue of the available infrastructure. The city will feature total water cycle management, including aquifer recharge, storm water and wastewater reuse. Advanced energy saving and environmental systems will be built into residential and commercial buildings. Foreign investors are invited to participate in this project.

Cooperative Research Centres

In May 1990, the federal government launched a programme to support long-term, high quality scientific and technological research. This programme was called the Cooperative Research Centres Program (CRC). Under the CRC programme, collaborative research ventures were established between universities, the public sector and the business world to undertake specific technological projects. Foreign involvement is one of the objectives of the programme.

At the end of 1996, 62 Cooperative Research Centres were operating in Australia. These projects spanned a range of disciplines—manufacturing technology, information and communication technology, mining and energy, agriculture, environment, and medical science.

The CRC programme is administered by the federal Department of Industry, Science and Tourism. Additional information can be obtained from the CRC Association, through which the various CRC members network and conduct programmes for the benefit of its members.

The Environment

Australia is the second driest continent after Antarctica. At an average 28 degrees latitude from the equator, the country is centred in the planet's low rainfall region between the higher rainfall temperate zones and the tropics. This is the region where deserts occur in both the Northern and Southern Hemispheres.

With the lowest average height above sea level among the world's continents, Australia lacks the mountain ranges that help generate rainfall on other continents. Mount Kosciusko (2,228 m), the country's highest peak, is a modest affair compared to the great mountains of the Himalayas, the Rockies, the Andes and the Alps.

More than one-third of Australia receives less than 250 mm rainfall per year and another third receives between 250 mm to 500 mm—conditions that are generally defined as arid and semi-arid respectively.

Not only is the average rainfall low, but the climate is highly variable and prone to periodic droughts caused by the so called Southern Oscillation in the eastern half of the country. This phenomenon links the climate in Eastern Australia to the periodic and unpredictable warming of the Pacific Ocean off the western shores of South America—known as the El Niño condition. El Niño raises atmospheric pressure around the Australian east coast, creating a series of "blocking highs" that prevent rain-bearing depressions from entering the weather system from the west. Droughts in Eastern Australia last until El Niño dies down. The worst of such droughts can persist for five to seven years.

Geologically stable, Australia is the oldest continent in the world. As a result, Australian soils are amongst the world's most unproductive, having been leached of nutrients by prolonged weathering and having a low rate of soil formation due to aridity. Australian ecology is fragile. After 200 years of European agriculture, Australia's rate of soil removal due to erosion is many times its natural rate of formation. Less than 10% of the continental area has soil of sufficient fertility to sustain intensive agriculture.

As an isolated continent in the Southern Hemisphere, Australia is relatively free from the environmental depredations of neighbouring countries. No upstream countries pollute its river systems. With the notable exception of the southern ozone hole, the environmental problems that Australia does experience are of its own making and therefore, can be solved by its own actions.

Favourable Areas

In some areas, the Australian environment is in relatively good condition by world standards. Australians are one of the most environmentally-conscious people in the world. The listing of natural areas under the World Heritage Convention has been effective in preserving habitat. Almost all town water is of potable quality, though some of the more remote towns cannot lay claim to this. Food standards are good. Solid waste recycling programmes have been successful and the countryside and coastal areas are relatively unpolluted.

Problem Areas

The 1996 State of the Environment Report prepared on behalf of the federal Ministry for the Environment identified the loss of biodiversity, degradation of the water supply and land degradation as major environmental problems internal to the country.

Loss of biodiversity has occurred principally from loss of habitat, whether it be wetlands, mangroves, bush land or rainforest. Loss of habitat is particularly difficult to control because it arises from the disparate actions of a multitude of uncoordinated authorities through such activities as agriculture, urban development, road construction, wood chipping and mining. In addition, in a society where decisions are made principally on short-term economic considerations, making an economic case for maintaining habitat is difficult.

Degradation of the water supply is a consequence of aridity. Rainfall in Australia is a limiting resource. Presently, surface water is being supplemented with ground-water taken from the Great Artesian Basin, which underlies about 22% of the continent. In fact, 60% of the country depends entirely on ground-water and in a further 20% of the land area, ground-water comprises more than half of the total water demand.

Ground-water is, however, a diminishing resource that is being withdrawn much faster than its replenishment rate. Water taken from bores is from the rain that fell one to two million years ago. Much of this water is carelessly used. For example, the residents of Perth, who derive 40% of their water supply from ground-water, liberally sprinkle their gardens of European plants, which are totally unsuited to the hot dry summers of the city.

A problem that is common to both water and land degradation is salinity—the result of rising water tables bringing dissolved salts to the surface. The phenomenon of man-made salinity and land degradation caused by land clearance and irrigation in arid areas is neither new nor unique to Australia. The present salt marshes of Iraq were once the Mesopotamian cradle of agriculture and the deserts of Mexico were once forests. Over a few hundred years, the Easter Islander civilisation, which inhabited the planet a thousand years ago, logged and farmed itself first into starvation, then into oblivion.

The salination of Australian agricultural areas is not yet complete. Water tables in some parts of the country are presently rising at a rate of 0.5 m per year. One-third of the irrigation area in Victoria has already been salinised, and about half the agricultural area of Western Australia will be under threat in the next 30 years from land clearing activities conducted 30 years before. In some parts of the Murray-Darling Basin—Australia's largest water catchment area—the water table has risen by up to 30 m since 1880. In some country towns such as Wagga Wagga in

An inland salt lake in South Australia—the result of rising water tables in Australia.

New South Wales, salination has invaded urban areas, undermining the foundations of houses by destroying their brick footings.

Government Action

Australia had the first Green political party in the world. On 23 March 1972, the United Tasmania Group was formed to stop the construction of a hydroelectric dam that would have inundated the surrounds of Lake Pedder in south western Tasmania. This political action failed but in 1984 the United Tasmania Group succeeded in a similar campaign to prevent the damming of the Franklin River.

In recent years, the Green Party has succeeded in having a number of candidates elected to the federal Senate, where they exercise considerable influence. After all, the combination of minority party members and independents hold the balance of power in the Senate.

Successive governments are torn between their stated policies to take a long-term view of the environment and appeasing commercial interests, whose main preoccupation is maximising profits. In 1992, the government agreed to the National Strategy for Ecologically Sustainable Development (ESD). Similar strategies were adopted by over 150 other countries at the UN Conference on Environment and Development. Sustainable development was defined as the effort to meet the needs of the present population without compromising those of the future generations.

Government responsibility for the environment is shared between federal, state and local governments, and the community. A crucial problem is the lack of a single administering authority in tackling vital environmental issues on a national basis. However, for many years, the various governments have managed to coordinate their efforts in some areas. An example is the creation of the Murray-Darling Basin Commission to coordinate and manage Australia's major water catchment area.

The single biggest environmental problem is land clearing in its various forms. Land clearing simultaneously contributes to all the main environmental problems, namely the loss of habitat that causes loss of biodiversity, rising water tables that cause salinity, increasing erosion that causes land degradation, and increasing greenhouse gas emissions that cause global warming.

Australia's scientifically-aware farmers have become more conscious of sustainable land use practices in recent years. The government's Landcare programme to plant trees and hedgerows has been influential at the individual level. Other actions by the governments, such as the Better Cities programme, has successfully promoted recycling and resource efficiency.

There is some evidence to suggest that the changing of billing procedures to include water and sewage invoices based on measured and estimated volumes is having an effect on the reduction of domestic demand for these resources.

On the other hand, the privatisation of the electricity industry is likely to have the opposite effect on greenhouse gas emissions. Working under fixed price regimes, the most obvious way for privately-owned utilities to increase profits is to promote increased consumption.

The Environment versus the Economy
In November 1995, Texas Utilities was the successful bidder for Eastern Energy, the electrical distribution system in Melbourne's eastern suburbs. The price Texas Utilities paid was much higher than most economists expected. When quizzed about how he intended to get his money back, the Texas spokesman, Dan Farrell, said that the company saw potential for growth, pointing out that houses in Melbourne use 40% less energy than comparable houses in Texas. Environmentalists interpreted this statement as an intention to abandon the government's previous drive for increased efficiency and reduced greenhouse gas emissions.

Source: *The Age*, 8 November 1995

International Issues
Outside the strictly domestic environment, there are issues such as global warming, ozone depletion and degradation of oceans, which all nations must play a part in solving.

In accordance with the Montreal Protocol of 1987, all industrial nations have cooperated in protecting the ozone layer by banning the use and manufacture of chlorofluorocarbons (CFCs). Australia exceeded its Montreal commitments by phasing out CFCs faster than required under its Protocol obligations. Also strongly supported by Australia was The New Fisheries Act, which was introduced to reduce the pressure on fish stocks in response to global concern about the depletion of oceans.

These acts of good global citizenship contrast with Australia's performance on global warming—perhaps the most insidiously serious environmental problem of all. While Australia was one of the 178 countries to commit to the environmental reforms of the 1992 Earth Summit in Rio de Janeiro, it is well short of meeting its commitment to return to the 1990 levels of greenhouse gas emissions. Australia is the world's second largest greenhouse gas emitter per capita. Furthermore, the rate of emission is rising at a time when it is meant to fall. Many simple measures, such as legislation for improved insulation and the installation of solar domestic water heating, are being ignored, as is development of renewable energy technologies.

The control of greenhouse gas emissions in Australia faces the usual intergovernmental conflicts. No one agency is in charge of fixing the problem. The largest individual contributor to greenhouse gas emissions is land clearance (27% of the total), an activity that is spread across the entire economy but particularly favoured by the politically powerful agricultural lobby. Other large contributions come from power generation—which is largely outside government control since many power companies are now privatised—and vehicles—whose numbers are mainly influenced by the actions of state governments in building roads and/or providing public transport.

The prospect of linking trade and performance of environment commitments is being studied by a committee of the World Trade Organisation (WTO). This raises the possibility that agreed greenhouse emission levels may be imposed upon exporting countries in the 21st century.

US President Bill Clinton, in his 1997 visit to Australia, made an impassioned speech on the subject in Cairns, pointing out the risks of global warming to future generations. Furthermore, the US State Department has declared that it will seek Japan's agreement to implement "enforceable" trade sanctions against countries who do not meet their greenhouse commitments.

The likelihood is that, sooner or later, Australia may have to face up to the environmental standards for greenhouse gas emissions set by the rest of the world, whether the Australian Government agrees with them or not. Unless it does so, failure to meet its greenhouse commitments may pose some risk to Australia's future ability to trade with the rest of the world

Opportunities for "Green" Products

Although some sections of the Australian business community, such as the powerful mining lobby, oppose the Green movement, others see proposals to adopt environmentally-friendly practices as an opportunity to develop markets for innovative environmentally-friendly products and technologies.

One environmentally beneficial measure that can be taken is the co-generation of power, whereby electricity is generated from heat created by the waste products of industrial processes, then sold back to the grid. Co-generation is less developed in Australia than other nations. For example, Holland gets 30% of its electricity through co-generation.

Attitudes of the various governments in Australia to the promotion of environmentally-friendly practices varies with the party and sentiment of those in power. Victoria is probably the most environmentally-hostile of all the states. Victoria, as leader of the movement to privatise public assets, has legislated to prohibit co-generation, with the objective of making power generating utilities more attractive business packages. (The more power they generate, the more money the utilities make. Conservation measures such as co-generation would take some demand from the privatised utilities.)

On the other hand, in other states, several government-sponsored renewable energy projects are under way. Western Australia has had a wind farm at Esperance on the southern coast of the state for a number of years. South Australia is installing a 4.5 kW solar station for an isolated tourist resort at a place called

Wipena Pound. At the same time, New South Wales is installing wind turbines and solar power generators in various locations. Solar water heating manufacturing is an established industry in Australia with exports into nearby countries such as the Philippines, which has been the recent party to a $40 million contract with a commercial company, BR Solar Australia, for the provision of electricity to 400 villages in the Philippines.

Summary of Environmental Opportunities
Australia is already at the forefront of several environmentally-friendly technologies such as solar power. Science, highly developed in the country, is greatly focused on environmental projects. At the federal level, the government is likely to come under increasing pressure to comply with globally accepted environmental standards. With its natural advantages, Australia may be an ideal location for investors who want to participate in the development of environmental products.

CHAPTER 5

Setting Up Business in Australia

Overview
Setting up business in Australia is a relatively quick and painless process. Foreign business is welcome in Australia and no discriminatory practices will be imposed on foreign investors setting up shop in the country. In some circumstances, financial and other assistance may be available.

Rules for Incorporation
Any foreign business that is already incorporated in its country of origin can establish a branch in Australia without registering as an Australian company. The investor may also wish to incorporate an Australian company or take over all or part of an existing Australian company. Whatever the preferred option, the foreign business or business person must file the correct paperwork with Australia's corporate regulatory authority.

Australian Securities Commission (ASC)
Regulation of companies passed from state to federal government control in about 1990. The central registry for companies is now the Australian Securities Commission (ASC).

Vestiges of state legislation remain for some special forms of corporate structures such as partnerships and trusts, for which different laws may apply in different states. Investors setting up more exotic corporate structures should first check state registration requirements with an accountant in the intended state of incorporation.

If the investor decides to form an Australian company, a limited choice of corporate arrangements is available, one of which will most likely suit the activity the enterprise is engaged in. A commercial entity in Australia may trade as a company, a partnership, a sole proprietor or as some form of trust. A company can be registered over the Internet with the assistance of companies specialising in corporate formation.

Australia's Millionth Company
In April 1997, Australia's millionth company was registered with the ASC. The millionth company, which received a special plaque to mark the occasion, was curiously enough, 100% foreign-owned. The company, Australian Color World PetroChemical Company Pty Ltd, had, as its equal shareholders and directors, two Chinese businessmen resident in Hong Kong

In its 1997 yearbook, the Australian Bureau of Statistics estimated that there were 932,000 private sector businesses actively operating in Australia.

Forms of Corporate Structure

Limited Liability Company
The most common corporate arrangement is a limited liability company which may be fully owned by the investor or jointly owned by the investor and outside shareholders. Two types of limited liability company exist: the *public* limited liability company and the *proprietary* limited liability company.

The public limited liability company

- Invites the public to buy shares under a prospectus detailing the intended use of the funds
- Must have a minimum of five shareholders
- Must have a minimum of five directors

The proprietary limited company

- Cannot invite the public to buy shares
- Cannot indirectly invite the public to subscribe to equity by issuing shares to corporations that are themselves publicly owned
- May have any number of shareholders down to a minimum of one shareholder
- May have any number of directors down to a minimum of one director

Under ASC regulations, a limited company must have the word *Limited* (usually abbreviated to "Ltd") as the last word in its name. Likewise, a proprietary company must have the words *Proprietary Limited* (usually abbreviated to "Pty Ltd") as the last two words in its name.

BHP

The only exception to this rule is Broken Hill Proprietary Company Limited (BHP), Australia's biggest company. The formation of BHP predated the 1864 legislation that reserved the word *proprietary* for the names of private companies. At the time, BHP, which was widely identified by the phrase "The Proprietary", felt its public identity would be damaged if the name of the company was changed. As a consequence, BHP obtained special dispensation to retain the word *Proprietary* in its company name.

Source: Alan Trengrove, *What's Good for Australia ...! The Story of BHP*

Once the company is registered, it is issued a nine-digit Australian Company Number (ACN) that, under ASC regulations, must be displayed on all corporate paperwork such as letterhead stationery, purchase orders, invoices, statements and the like.

Partnerships

Partnerships are a prevalent form of business structure in some industries, especially professional associations like law and accounting, where professional work is charged by the hour and there is no physical output. A principal disadvantage of a partnership is that there is no legal liability: all partners are liable for the debts of the other partners without limitation.

Partnership law does not preclude foreign partners. In addition, partners can be domestic or foreign corporations rather than merely individuals.

Sole Proprietorship

A sole proprietorship is a commercial organisation similar to a limited liability company but run by a single individual. Sole proprietorships are usually restricted to small businesses that are run by the owners themselves.

Trusts

A trust is a special corporate structure where affairs are run at arm's length by an administrator termed a *trustee*. This is a more complicated administrative arrangement but carries two principal benefits. Firstly, the tax burden of the beneficiaries of the trust can be reduced because the income can be split amongst unit-holders in any proportion to suit their individual tax positions. Secondly, the trust can be set up in such a way as to minimise the exposure of the proprietors of the enterprise to litigation. Many politicians and other highly paid individuals operate trusts, which are structured by accounting firms specialising in trust formation to suit the investor's individual circumstances.

Branch of Foreign Company

If an incorporated foreign company wishes to trade under its own name in Australia, it can legally do so, provided it first registers with the Australian Securities Commission. To register, the foreign company must submit details of its domestic incorporation documentation to the ASC. If not already in the English language, the documents must be translated. Once the foreign company is registered in Australia, the ASC will issue an identifying number (the Australian Registered Body Number or ARBN), which operates in a similar manner as the ACN issued for incorporated companies. Under ASC regulations, the ARBN must be included on all commercial documents that the company uses within Australia, such as letterhead stationery, invoices and purchase orders.

Franchising

Franchising is the structure chosen by many small businesses. People making the switch from salaried employment to self employment may find undertaking a franchise operation a smaller step to take. This is because the franchiser makes many of the business decisions by presenting the franchisee with a ready-made product and market. On the downside, franchisees have less leeway to make their own decisions and must pay fees to the franchiser. Australian business, particularly retailing, presents opportunities for foreign franchisers. Franchising has a healthy growth rate in a country where an increasing number of people, retrenched from salaried occupations, are striking out in businesses of their own.

Level of Franchising in 1996

Turnover of franchising businesses	$50 billion
Number of franchisers	500
Number of franchisees	26,000
Number of people employed in franchising	280,000
Five-year average annual growth rate	12%

Statistics over a number of years show that small business franchises are two and a half times less likely to fail than nonfranchise small businesses. The fast food chain, McDonald's, is the largest franchise operation in the country.

Joint Ventures

Some foreign investors may wish to operate independently without an Australian partner. Others may wish to form Australian-registered companies, with Australian individuals or corporations as shareholders.

A third course is to set up a joint venture in which the foreign investor becomes involved with one or more local firms to undertake a particular project while both parties maintain their existing corporate structures. This arrangement is particularly applicable if the investment is short-term such as a construction project with a definite completion date after which involvement of the two contracting parties serves no further purpose.

Having decided to set up a joint venture, both parties will want to draw up a written agreement. Contracts in Australia are considered binding; therefore it is important to ensure that the clauses in the contract reflect mutual intentions so that future misunderstanding between contracting parties are avoided.

Steps in Forming the Company

Corporate registration has been greatly simplified since responsibility for corporate affairs was assumed by ASC. The ASC requires the submission of only a minimal amount of information.

Information required for submission when registering a company in Australia:

- Proposed name of the company
- Proposed registered office
- Principal place of doing business (may be the same as the registered office)
- Name and address of directors
- Name and address of secretary (who may also be a director)

Note that the forms on which these information are to be submitted are the ASC Forms 201 and 21. These two forms (accompanied by a fee of about $700) are submitted in person to the ASC—usually by an agent of the company's accountant—and will normally be approved on the spot. Using accounting firms specialising in this sort of activity, the incorporation documents can be prepared and the company can be registered and ready for business within a few hours.

The only restriction on company name, other than the normal bounds of good taste, is that the company may not have a name already allocated to another company. Historically, company names that were similar to other companies would not be approved. However, this restriction has since been relaxed. Now, companies are identified principally by their ACN.

After the company name is registered, an accountant will normally be hired to prepare the rest of the documentation such as the Memorandum of Association and the Articles of Association.

On-going Obligations of a Business
Requirements for businesses to submit reports to regulatory authorities have been greatly reduced in recent years.

Proprietary Limited Liability Companies
Preparation of audited financial accounts can be waived by the unanimous agreement of shareholders. Most private businesses take advantage of this waiver to save themselves the time and expense of audit. The absolute minimum information proprietary limited liability companies are obliged to submit to the ASC each year is the identities of directors and shareholders.

However, even if shareholders agree to waive auditing of accounts, companies must still submit annual accounts to the taxation office. This is not such an onerous task, as taxation returns are done by self-assessment. Audited accounts are not required. Any subsequent tax audit will be conducted by the tax office at its expense. This is, however, unusual as the tax department only audits about 2% of returns.

Public Limited Liability Companies
A public limited liability company, on the other hand, does not have the right to waive the preparation of audited accounts. Obligations to protect shareholders are greater for public companies. Annual financial statements, properly audited by an independent auditor, must be submitted to the ASC.

Responsibilities of Directors
Under Australian law, all companies must have a board of directors, even if, in the case of proprietary limited liability companies, the board may comprise only one individual. Directors are appointed to the company's board on a simple majority vote by shareholders.

Often, for proprietary limited liability companies, shareholders and directors can be the same individuals. For public limited liability companies, directors are generally salaried business people who may or may not hold shares in the companies on whose boards they sit.

The ASC also requires the appointment of a secretary, who may or may not be a director, and a public officer, who is responsible for taxation returns. Once again, for proprietary limited liability companies, these may or may not be the same person.

Directors and the office bearers of the company are appointed and/or reappointed by shareholders once a year at the company's annual general meeting.

Traditionally, the fundamental obligation of directors is to run the company in the interests of the shareholders. This responsibility imposes minimum ethical standards.

In recent years, the legal responsibilities of directors in Australia have widened as a result of a number of court cases involving disgruntled shareholders, creditors, employees and others. For example, directors can be personally responsible for

> **Directors' Duties**
> The duties of directors are to:
>
> - Act for the benefit of the company on whose board they sit
> - Take due care and diligence
> - Act honestly
> - Avoid conflicts of interest
> - Avoid using information acquired as a director for personal gain or other improper purpose
>
> Source: *Director's Toolkit*, KPMG

the company's debts if a company fails after trading while insolvent. The chairperson of the board, in particular, has a duty to discharge his or her responsibilities as director.

In addition, directors have legal obligations outside their duties to shareholders, employees and creditors for the performance of the company. Obligations to the world at large relate to areas such as customs and excise, environmental protection, industrial relations, occupational health and safety, stock exchange listing rules, taxation laws and trade practices/consumer affairs.

In reality, though these laws exist, issues regarding ethical behaviour rarely arise. Even blatant conflict of interest issues are often not brought to court. No case of insider trading has ever been successfully prosecuted in Australia.

Agency Agreements

Import Agents
A company exporting goods into Australia may wish to establish an enterprise under its own name in Australia or appoint an Australian agent to market its goods and services. Selling imported goods is a major industry in Australia. Australian importers are constantly on the lookout for new products to sell. Lists of

prospective agents can be obtained through various databases such as Austrade, the Internet or even the *Yellow Pages* phone book. Some agents require an exclusive franchise for your product while others do not. If a franchise is granted, make sure it is for a limited trial period, with options for extension if sales are satisfactory.

Agents may be big or small companies. Both have their advantages and disadvantages.

Advantages of small companies as agents:

- Your product is likely to be sold by the business owner rather than a sales representative.
- There is likely to be more emphasis on your product as it may be part of a smaller catalogue and be more important to the agent.

Advantages of large companies as agents:

- The geographical area covered is likely to be large (travelling the long distances between Australian population centres is a significant business expense).
- These companies are more likely to have the financial resources needed to carry stocks.

A middle course is also available for increasing the geographical penetration of your product. You can carve up the country into administrative regions so that instead of appointing an agent for the whole country, an agent can be appointed for a group of states, for each state or even for regions within a state. Alternatively, an agent appointed for a major state can cover a smaller state as well. For example, an agent appointed for a populous state such as Victoria may also take care of Tasmania. Another version of the agency arrangement is to appoint an agent for the entire country and allow him or her to appoint sub-agents for the various states. A disadvantage of this approach is that the price of the goods is marked up at each step of the hierarchy.

One other note of advice. Insist that your agent puts his contact details on the brochures of your products and, if possible, on the products themselves. There are a staggering number of expensive glossy brochures circulating within Australia that lack this important piece of information. Such brochures may display to potential customers the exact product they wish to buy, but they will not know where to buy it.

Customs Agents

According to Australian customs procedures, goods have to be allocated to particular tariff categories before they are allowed into the country. To minimise the rate of duty, goods should be allocated to the tariff category bearing the lowest duty. While information on tariff categories and tariff rates is available from the Australian Customs Service, categories are constantly changing. In addition, Australian Customs presents the information in a form that is almost impossible for a non-specialist in the area to understand.

If you have appointed a sales and distribution agent to market your product in Australia, you should stipulate in the agency agreement that the agent bears full responsibility for getting your goods through the Australian Customs, including the payment of customs duty—if applicable. However, if you are an exporter who is direct selling to the Australian market, using a customs agent to get your goods off the wharf and through the Customs Department is essential. You can find a list of customs agents in the *Yellow Pages*.

Outside the complexity of paperwork, there is another reason for using customs agents. The waterfront (assuming the goods come in by ship) is an area that has proved resistant to microeconomic reform by the government. On the waterfront, informal "arrangements" can ease your goods through the system and into the country. However, neglect of these "arrangements" can increase the chances of your goods becoming lost or held up. Only custom agents know their way around this maze.

Raising Capital

The amount of capital that can be imported into Australia for legitimate investment is not restricted. To raise capital within Australia, options are available from either the private or public sectors. Businesses importing exclusive technology may seek a joint venture partner under a contract, where the local partner subscribes the capital in return for a share in the benefits of the technology. In other cases, local and foreign joint venture partners may subscribe expertise and capital in proportion to their shareholding.

Money market corporations (previously known as Merchant Banks) provide short- and long-term finance to approved borrowers as well as foreign exchange, currency hedging services, underwriting services and financial advisory services. In some instances, money market corporations may subscribe share equity, though this practice has become less prevalent since the stock market crash of the 1980s.

The financial services sector also provides lease financing, factoring and property development loans. Finance companies provide short- to medium-term financing and leasing principally to smaller businesses.

Trading banks provide overdrafts for working capital and fixed term loans or leases for capital expenditures. Banks usually require extensive collateral, particularly real estate, beyond the assets in the business. In addition, loans and overdraft facilities are often supported by directors' guarantees against discharge of the loan.

Though official government financing has become more difficult to obtain in recent years, a number of grant and loan schemes still exist, though these are mostly restricted to domestic companies or joint ventures with a high proportion of domestic ownership. For example, the Australian Industry Development Corporation (AIDC) will advance loans and take equity positions in undertakings that require capital—but undertakings with shareholders who are residents of Australia are preferred.

As well as the formal public money schemes, all layers of government—federal, state and local—may be prepared to enter into *ad hoc* deals with foreign businesses if they can be persuaded that the enterprise being established will benefit their own turf.

It can still be difficult for innovative small firms to get funds to develop new products, although the government has recently announced initiatives to help in this area through its Small Business Innovation Fund (SBIF) and R&D Start programme.

The business magazine, *Business Review Weekly* (BRW), has implemented a scheme to assist innovative firms in locating investors through a "dating service" called the Australian Equity Association, whereby prospective innovators and investors can make contact with one another. Contact is made between the parties via the BRW website where each party lists its requirements.

Stock Exchange
The largest source of capital for public and financial institutions is through the stock exchange. However, issuing shares on the stock exchange usually requires a reasonable history of profitable trading prior to listing. The stock exchange is thus not normally appropriate for the raising of initial capital for new ventures.

Until the mid-1980s, separate stock exchanges existed in the capital cities. These stock exchanges were then amalgamated and corporatised into a single authority, the Australian Stock Exchange Limited (ASX) that can be traded from anywhere in the country. The stock exchange is divided into two divisions—the main board of large companies and the second board of smaller companies.

Like markets the world over, 19 October 1987 was not a good day on the stock exchanges of Australia. In fact, the impact of the great global market crash of 1987 was felt more deeply in Australia than in most other countries. Recovery took longer. Whereas the Wall Street Dow Jones Index fell 22% after the crash and was trading back at its pre-crash level by 1990, the measure of the Australian Stock Exchange—the All Ordinaries Index—fell by half. The market peaked at 2306 on 23 September 1987. It went to a low of 1203 on 11 November 1987 and took almost 10 years to break the 2300 point barrier again.

Imprudent lending in the 1980s to a group that had become known simply by the title, "the entrepreneurs", damaged financial institutions when the 1987 crash occurred. The damage was greater in Australia than in the United States or Europe, where Australian-style entrepreneurship was less prominent. Australian merchant banks such as Rothwells and TriContinental were mortally wounded, and collapsed. Two building societies, Pyramid Building Society and Estate Mortgage, were wound up. Three major trading banks failed. Depositors of the ailing trading banks were bailed out when the government engineered takeovers by other banks.

After the crash, all the four major banks carried large portfolios of non-performing loans to the failed entrepreneurs. Most of these loans were quietly retired over a five-year period from 1987 to 1993, dragging down profits for those years. Interestingly, the privately-owned banks, ANZ and Westpac, whose managers had wider discretionary limits and far higher salaries, performed much worse than the government-owned Commonwealth Bank. The National Bank of Australia emerged from the crash in better shape than the other two private banks, cementing its position as the number one bank in the country.

In the late 1980s and early 1990s, banks returned to a bricks-and-mortar mentality but this was not totally successful either—in that period, even bricks and mortar lost money. The aftermath of the stock market crash has left an enduring mark of caution on the financial sector. Today, private sector capital to fund innovation is difficult to get and bankers are more reluctant to extend loans for projects like product development programmes since these are seen as risky.

"The Entrepreneurs"

A number of individualistic businessmen dominated the Australian economy in the mid-1980s, creating business empires funded by massive debts that were used to finance not only business operations, but also opulent personal lifestyles.

The most prominent figure of all, Alan Bond, ran TV stations, imported Korean cars, manufactured boats and airships, built an entire city (Yanchep Sun City in Western Australia), orchestrated Europe's largest property development in Rome, bought breweries in the United States, purchased an entire country village (Plympton) in the English countryside, paid the world's highest price ever for a work of art (US$50 million for Van Gogh's *Irises*) and won the 1983 America's Cup yacht race with the radically designed 12 m class yacht, *Australia II*. In 1988, the total debts of companies controlled by Bond—who was subsequently declared bankrupt—accounted for 6% of Australia's National Debt.

Other entrepreneurs were not far behind. Christopher Skase of Quintex put in a bid to buy MGM studios in Hollywood. Robert Holmes a Court obtained a controlling interest in Texaco, one of the world's major oil companies. Foster's Brewing was "fosterising" the planet, acquiring half the pubs in Britain and buying breweries in Canada, China and Romania. Australian businessmen (all of them were men) were out and about, taking over the world.

The Australian press in the 1980s had a love affair with its entrepreneurs and this flowed onto the general public. Aussie corporate heroes were just ordinary blokes—many of them not especially well-educated—who were prepared to "have a go" in the finest Aussie tradition.

It was a personality cult that the media reinforced. Financial reporters writing for the country's leading newspapers described multimillion dollar companies as if they were the personal playthings of their CEOs. Publicly-listed companies belonging to thousands of shareholders and employing thousands of employees were referred to as Bruce Judge's "Ariadne" or John Spalvins's "Adelaide Steamship" as if the other shareholders and employees did not exist.

The entrepreneurs acquired celebrity status. Papers published human interest stories about their mansions, art collections, limousines and executive jets, their tireless jetsetting and their wives and mistresses. This was a real life "Dynasty" played out by real people and best of all, with real money.

The hero-worshipping of the entrepreneurs flowed over to the banking industry, which abandoned its normal prudence. Bank executives fell over one another to lend these nascent national heroes billions of dollars in interest-bearing loans collateralised by no physical assets. Come the crash, paper corporations of the entrepreneurs blew away like straws in the wind, taking the bank loans with them.

After the crash, individuals lauded in the press the year before as "corporate heroes" found themselves dubbed "corporate cowboys". True to their new identity, a number of them unhitched their horses and skipped town, taking up residence in countries such as Spain and Poland, with which Australia had no extradition treaty arrangements. Others such as Alan Bond stoically stayed in Australia and eventually faced various civil charges for some of his more unconventional commercial activities. Bond Corporation was liquidated some years later with creditors getting 0.5 cents in the dollar. Bond was charged with fraud. At his trial, he was sentenced to four years' jail, with the threat of trials to follow for alleged further felonies.

Those who escaped the debacles of the 1980s and did not have to slink away to Spain or Poland were the six-figure salary banking executives responsible for fuelling the debt binge. In the 1980s, the banking industry cost shareholders, depositors and taxpayers $25 billion in written-off loans that mostly violated lending guidelines. However, none of the CEOs of the major players had to take a pay cut, do time in jail or retire from his job.

Some time later, when the dust had settled after the crash, the Australian business magazine, *Business Review Weekly*, carried an article entitled "Wasters of the Universe", in which it calculated how much each of entrepreneurs had cost the community. The first five entrants on the list in order of the size of their losses were Alan Bond ($5.3 billion), Tim Marcus Clark—State Bank of South Australia ($3 billion), Ian Johns—State Bank of Victoria ($2.1 billion), John Elliott—Fosters Brewing ($1.5 billion) and Christopher Skase—Quintex ($1.25 billion).

In the 1990s, the stock exchange recovered. One of the effects was a substantial flow of ownership overseas. By 1996, approximately one-third of the value of the shares listed on the stock exchange was owned by foreigners.

Futures Market

In addition to the stock market (often referred to as the *physical market*), Australia has the Sydney Futures Market (SFE), which trade futures contracts in wool, live cattle, bank bills, the Australian Share Price Index (called the All Ordinaries Index) and government bonds. In addition, the market trades share price options. After-hours dealing is available through the Sydney Computerised Overnight Market (SYCOM), which is soon to be integrated with the worldwide futures market through Globex.

Tariffs

Until the mid-1960s, Australian industry was protected by fairly high tariff barriers. At that time, the currency was strong[1] and the balance of payments was in surplus. On the other hand, inflation was high and industrial productivity was not increasing as fast as it did in other countries. The government of the day felt that economic circumstances warranted a reduction in tariffs.

Tariffs rose and fell during the 1970s and 1980s, varying with the sentiment of the government in power. As world trade increased and trade blocs developed, the pressure to lower tariffs worldwide intensified. Today, while tariffs still exist for many items, Australian tariffs are low by international standards and likely to go lower still. The average rate of Australian tariffs on all imported items in 1996 was under 4%.

A debate rages between various interest groups with regards to the correct level of tariffs. An odd alliance exists between economic rationalists and the agricultural community, who are pressing for all tariffs to be reduced to zero. On the other hand, the manufacturing sector lobbies for existing tariff levels to be maintained. No group in the community is pressing for tariffs to be *increased*.

Why Reduce Tariffs?
Both the mining and agricultural lobbies are in favour of freeing up international trade. The reduction of tariffs presents several benefits to them, namely:

- The adoption of free trade principles strengthens Australia's moral position in objecting to market restrictions on primary products such as those operating in the EC.
- The prices of goods that are cost inputs to the primary industries will be lowered.
- Mining companies* and farmers enjoy seeing the Australian dollar depreciate. Under a lower tariff regime, more imported goods will be bought and sold. This will worsen the current account deficit—in turn putting pressure on the Australian dollar, which will increase Australian dollar revenue to commodities producers. This is because virtually all contracts for the supply of commodities are written in international currencies—predominantly the US dollar.

* Australia's biggest mining company is Broken Hill Pty Ltd. (BHP). Commenting on the March 1997 quarterly accounts, a BHP spokesperson remarked that every one cent rise in the Australian dollar (in relation to the US dollar) cost the company \$360 million bottom line annual profits.

In addition to the pressure of lobby groups, the government has an international political imperative to reduce tariffs in accordance with commitments made at the Uruguay Round of the WTO.

Anti-dumping
Australia is a party to world trade agreements on anti-dumping. Australian domestic industries which believe that dumped or

subsidised goods are damaging their market can voice their objections to the Australian Customs Service (ACS).

Dumped and Subsidised Goods
Dumped goods are defined as goods which are priced lower in the country into which they are exported than in their country of origin. Subsidised goods are defined as goods which are subsidised by the government of the exporting country.

If the verdict of the ACS is in favour of the local industry lodging the objection, additional duty will be levied on the importer at the difference between the dumped price of the goods and their domestic price in the country of origin. In the case of subsidised goods, additional duty will be levied at the amount of the subsidy paid in the country of origin.

Australian Legal System

Australian law originated as English law adopted in colonial times. Some laws from this time have remained in the statute books close to their original form. However, over the years, the body of Australian law has been added to and modified by statutes drafted in Australia.

There are nine lawmaking bodies in the country—the federal government, the six state governments and the governments of the two territories.

An Australian courtroom looks and operates much like its English counterpart. Judges and barristers in court still wear wigs and gowns. Court functionaries wear archaic costumes and bear archaic titles such as "tipstaff". In the case of trial by jury, a panel of 12 citizens sits in judgement.

Foreigners who decide to establish a relationship with another company will become a party to a contract at an early stage of proceedings—e.g., a joint venture agreement, an agency contract

To Wig or Not to Wig?
In 1997, members of the Victorian Bar Council voted on a proposal to abandon the practice of wearing wigs and robes in court. Despite the fact that a horsehair wig with its prescribed quantity of tails and curls costs $1,000, the proposal failed by a vote of two to one. Barristers, who charge their clients from $1,000 to $5,000 for their day in court, like the law the way it is.

or a contract with the government. Whatever the details of the arrangement, a legal agreement reflecting the terms of the contract will be prepared. For this, the services of a lawyer will be needed.

One of the 19th century traditions of English law was that fees for preparing legal agreements were charged by the number of words in the document. This tradition still persists in Australian law. As a result, many Australian lawyers are inclined to prepare legal documents in archaic and circumlocutory language in order to increase their length and therefore the amount that can be invoiced. This form of English expression, somewhat irreverently called *legalese*, is particularly unsuited to, say, a foreign business person from a non-English-speaking country, to whom English is a second language. In fact, it is fair to say that even most English-speaking people make little effort to understand legal documents even though they are written in their mother tongue. Standard practice is to seek help from a solicitor.

While the government has declared its intentions to reduce the law to "plain English", the legal industry, which derives much of its revenue from endless interpretations of obscure legal terminology, has displayed little enthusiasm for the task.

It is important to remember, in dealings between clients and lawyers, that the client is running the relationship. The lawyer is merely a hired hand. There is no need for anyone entering a contract to tolerate the legalese that some lawyers produce as a matter of habit. Plain English legal documents have equal weight in law and are less likely to contain mistakes. Therefore, if a contract prepared for your signature contains a term you do not understand, instruct the lawyer to have it written in simpler terms.

In Australia, parties to contracts will be expected to comply completely with any contract they make. This puts an obligation on those drafting the contract to get it right from the start. On this topic, investors should beware of lawyers representing the other party to the contract—they are likely to introduce additional clauses into the final contract that were not part of the preliminary negotiations. No one should sign anything they are not happy with. Remember that once a contract has been signed, it is binding.

Like other professions, lawyers specialise in particular disciplines. Each state has a controlling body—the Law Institute (the exact name varies from one state to another)—for lawyers operating within that state. For prospective business people who have no existing arrangements with lawyers, the Law Institute can provide a recommended list of at least three lawyers suited to your particular task.

Lawyers are assiduous about billing every hour of their day to clients. True to this tradition—unlike the associations of other trades or professions—the Law Institute will bill you for their referral service.

Fees of lawyers vary with the matter being treated and, in particular, with the lawyer's address. A city lawyer may charge twice as much as one from out of town. The fee charged does not necessarily correlate with talent, though corporate law specialists with city addresses tend to be expensive. Lawyers almost invariably charge by the hour, or to be more precise, by fractions of an hour.

Unlike other commercial operations, few lawyers will quote lump sum prices for the work they undertake. Some may provide an estimate of costs but this can normally be disregarded. Lawyers think nothing of exceeding their estimates by 300% or 400% when the time comes to present the bill. When using a lawyer over a long period of protracted negotiations, it is wise to request frequent

Lawyers' Fees

To calculate fees, many lawyers use a decimal time system. They divide each hour up into six minute segments—each equivalent to one-tenth of an hour. They will then bill their aggregate hours to the nearest decimal point. Lawyers are also exacting about charging for every office overhead they use—almost down to the paper clips. For example, every phone call made or every sheet of paper photocopied may be charged to the client, often at an exorbitant rate. The bill first presented will usually reflect only the total amount. However, clients are entitled to a detailed bill if they request it. Remember, though, that in the event of a request for a detailed bill, lawyers may charge for the time taken to list the detail, even if doing so exposes some error in their original billing!

updates of the billing. You should also keep meticulous notes of the details, dates and times of conversations with lawyers so that when the lawyer's time is later charged on the bill, you can check the billing against your own records.

To minimise the cost of preparing legal documents, present to your lawyer the essence of the agreement in as much detail as possible. For this, you will need to have developed a clear idea of what you want. The worst approach is to assume a lawyer can read your mind.

Summary

In the true traditions of a free and casual society, Australia is one of the easiest countries in which to do business. Business setup costs are minimal and a new business can be registered with ASC, and be up and running in less than one working day. In fact, a business can even be set up from overseas through an accounting firm specialising in this field (some interchange of signed documents would be required). Although some additional restrictions on business activities were imposed after "the entrepreneur" episode, government regulation of business has been relaxed. Government policy today encourages foreign investment by presenting the fewest possible barriers.

CHAPTER 6

Business Operations

Overview

Once an investor decides to establish a business in Australia, a location must be selected. The general standard of facilities offered does not vary greatly across the country. However, like businesses do tend to congregate in certain geographical locations, depending on the resources required. Steel-making, for example, has traditionally been located on the east coast near the Bulli and Hunter Valley coalfields. Chemical plants have located in Kernell in Sydney or Altona on the western fringes of Melbourne. Mining industries locate near the ore bodies.

Costs of doing business vary slightly from one state to another, and between one region and another. Costs associated with property, such as rentals and freehold prices, are generally higher in Sydney than elsewhere. Property costs are generally a little higher in most capital cities than in surrounding provincial areas. Against this, infrastructure and the availability of services in cities are commensurately better.

The preferred location of any new business is driven by a wide range of considerations like the access to markets and suppliers, the availability of labour and the availability of investment incentives.

Location

Setting Up

Business premises available in Australia can range from a one-room tenanted office with a shared secretary/receptionist in a small complex to a green field site for factories and other developments. Premises may be bought or leased, depending on the situation. If the business requires a professional city address, the premises will almost certainly be rented space in a city high rise. The quality of city premises can range from premium spaces to disused warehouses. Rental costs vary accordingly.

A wide range of industrial premises is also available for lease, from *factoryettes* (where a site is subdivided into a number of factories sharing common access areas) to undeveloped land. The industry standard for lease terms in Australia is an initial three-year lease with options for the tenant to extend for two further three-year terms (leases termed by real estate agents as "three by three"). Prices may be fixed for the entire initial lease period or they may be based on a fixed rate subject to an annual Consumer Price Index (CPI) adjustment. Prices can also be fixed for one year and set at the "market price" thereafter. Rental costs for all grades of property in Australia are cheap by international standards.

Rental Costs for Premium Office Space, 1996

Location	$US	Index
Hong Kong	1,236	653
Singapore	1,018	538
Shanghai	741	392
Osaka	699	369
Los Angeles	394	208
Kuala Lumpur	341	180
Seoul	341	180
Stuttgart	286	151
Bangkok	277	146
Jakarta	247	131
Auckland	191	101
Melbourne	189	100

*Rental costs = US$ per sq m per annum.

Source: KPMG data provided by *Business Victoria*

The Melbourne business district has one of the cheapest rental costs in the world.

The majority of leases written for residential, industrial and commercial rental use "standard" lease terms. The standard lease is prepared by the Real Estate Institute of each state (and therefore may vary slightly between the states). Standard lease terms cover the rights and obligations of landlords and tenants, such as the rights of access, the rights to quiet enjoyment of space, rules on subleasing, etc.

The standard lease is thought to represent a fair balance between the rights of tenants and landlords. Use of a standard lease has a number of advantages. For a start, it saves the time, trouble and expense of preparing a lease from scratch. It is widely known, understood and tested by the real estate industry and lawyers who deal in property disputes. It is flexible since its conditions may, if circumstances warrant, be varied by writing out the general conditions of the lease with special conditions that relate to the arrangement being entered into. However, there is no legislation to prohibit landlords and tenants writing their own lease if they wish to do so.

For businesses which require factories, industrial parks throughout the country have ready-made factories for lease.

Alternatively, investors may prefer to purchase land for property development projects. A wide range of industrial sites is available near major cities. Industrial land in Australia is cheap compared to almost anywhere else in the world. Building construction costs are moderate.

Factory Development Cost—1996

Location	Land costs	Construction costs	Rental costs ($ per annum)
Osaka	2,239	1,119	269
Singapore	1,027	695	182
Hong Kong	560	1,260	1,400
Seoul	186	278	100
Stuttgart	265	794	67
Kuala Lumpur	204	377	67
Los Angeles	101	600	50
Bangkok	88	321	96
Auckland	86	424	67
Shanghai	86	734	51
Jakarta	81	200	79
Melbourne	28	322	44

*Land construction costs = US$ per sq m.

Source: KPMG data provided by *Business Victoria*

Note:
Development data is for the cost of a 4,000 sq m site within 20 km of a major port in a serviced industrial estate. Rental data is for a single floor area 2,000 sq m single span factory.

Fitting Out

Leased office property may be supplied with basic furnishings such as office furniture, fax and computer facilities or it may be leased as four bare walls that the lessee can fit out to his own requirements. If fixtures and fittings are required, these remain the property of the lessee and can be removed after the lease period, or left in the premises after negotiations with the landlord.

Taxation rules allow fittings such as building alterations or improvements—for example, office panelling—to be written off as a business expense in the year the expense is incurred. Except for low value items that can be written off immediately, office equipment must be depreciated at a rate determined by the Tax Office. For example, the allowable depreciation period for computer equipment is three years. Software, on the other hand, can be entirely written off in the year of its purchase. Low value equipment whose purchase price is less than $300 can be written off in the year of purchase, regardless of its nature.

Labour

Labour Availability

The standard of education in Australia is high by international standards. According to the 1996 employment statistics, the only skilled workers in short supply in the country are mathematicians and Japanese language teachers. Almost all other skills are in oversupply, both at the professional and trade level.

The standard of skilled labour produced by the apprenticeship system and the TAFE (Training and Further Education) Colleges is excellent. The workforce is generally flexible and most people possess skills outside their chosen discipline. In addition, almost everyone under 40 and most people over 40 are computer literate.

With persistent unemployment, a trend has developed where people will take any available job. Some young people will even work for nothing to gain the work experience that will help them in their future application for jobs. In most enterprises, skilled labour will almost certainly be available, particularly in the larger population centres such as the state capital cities.

Generally, the Australian workforce is well-trained and highly motivated. Australians are indiscriminate about the nationality of their employers.

Labour Relations

Historically, Australian labour earned an unenviable reputation for industrial disruption and disputation. In the past, this reputation was deserved. However, for various reasons, the level of industrial disruption by Australian labour has declined sharply in recent years.

During the 1970s and 1980s, more hours were lost to demarcation disputes than for any other reason. These disputes boiled down to squabbles between unions that the management of the industries involved were fairly powerless to resolve.

The Wirraway

Demarcation disputes in the Australian workforce used to be featured daily in the press. Ridiculous as the issues may seem, they can only be resolved by a hearing in the Industrial Court.

In 1982, the ship *Wirraway* sailed into Gladstone harbour in Queensland with a cargo of industrial products. A dispute erupted between members of the Seaman's Union and members of the Stevedore's Union as to which union was responsible for placing the vessel's mooring line over a bollard on the wharf. As a result, the *Wirraway* was stranded in the harbour with its unloaded cargo for four months until the dispute was resolved.

In the 1970s and 1980s, many in the community saw trade unions as a threat to society. But the union movement was self-destructing under the influence of fractious shop floor delegates, whom the management of unions could not control.

Labour problems peaked in the early 1980s. These were the last years of the Fraser Liberal government when the labour policies of both the government and labour unions was confrontational.

In 1983, the Labor government took office. The incoming prime minister, Bob Hawke, had previously held the position of President of the Australian Council of Trade Unions. Amongst those in power at the time, Hawke's understanding of the labour movement was unsurpassed. Upon his election, Hawke established a more consensual labour agenda than his predecessor. The government drew up a broad-based contract between the union movement and the new Labor government, which was embodied in an agreement called the Accord and was based on ideas of peaceful coexistence rather than militancy.

Over the last half of the 1980s and the first half of the 1990s, Australia saw an unprecedented decline in union power that still continues today. The institution of unionism has been assailed from all sides.

In 1988, the most militant union in the country, the Builders Labourers Federation, was declared in breach of the law and deregistered. Employment levels in union-dominated industries like manufacturing were in decline. The decentralisation of industry by privatisation reduced the ability of unions in government-run monopolies to hold the community to ransom by withdrawing essential services. The growth of the global economy has encouraged unions and members of unions to believe they are in competition with the world at large rather than local management.

Much of the Australian workforce has been fragmented by the contracting-out of services to the point of creating a new class of entrepreneurial trades people who see themselves as business people rather than workers. Though unions in a few industries attempt to run closed shops, union membership in Australia is not compulsory. As a percentage of the total workforce, union membership had in 1997 fallen to 31% from about 49.5% in 1982. It is still falling rapidly.

The decline in the power and activity of organised labour shows up strongly in national statistics of workdays lost to industrial disputation. In 1981, the number of workdays was 797 per thousand employees in the workforce. By 1990, the figure had fallen to 217 workdays lost per thousand employees.

Cost of Labour

Cost of labour in Australia is on the low end of the OECD scale, and in comparison to other countries, professional salaries in Australia are not high.

Professional Salaries in Australia—1996 figures

Location	Marketing Director	Accountant	Electronic Engineer	Process worker
Stuttgart	194,100	96,578	116,091	38,400
Osaka	190,547	119,508	101,978	33,348
Singapore	177,662	92,183	79,661	16,642
Hong Kong	143,773	91,116	56,907	16,335
Seoul	140,050	67,887	73,249	24,529
Los Angeles	138,696	88,670	90,180	30,979
Jakarta	118,910	41,412	47,550	2,362
Melbourne	116,560	57,412	66,634	20,095
Kuala Lumpur	116,006	40,602	41,891	5,223
Auckland	108,799	48,810	53,445	23,814
Bangkok	87,988	40,216	43,341	2,837
Shanghai	56,327	13,455	12,730	3,520

* Salaries = US$ per annum

Source: *Business Victoria*, KPMG

Wages and Salaries

In Australia, the minimum wage is set by legislation. The 1997 minimum wage for an unskilled adult worker was set at $9.50 per hour. Like other countries, there is a growing disparity between the rich and the poor in the workforce. In 1976, the bottom 20% of households received 4% of all income. By 1996, this figure had dropped to 1%.

These figures represent nothing more than changes in the relative bargaining power of participants in the labour market. The power of unionists has eroded and their relative wages are falling at an increasing rate. With the rise of globalisation, Australian workers are feeling the competition from the minimal wage rates and minimal labour laws of developing countries.

Investors calculating the costs of projects in Australia should note that additives should be applied to the basic hourly labour rate. The basic labour rate should be increased by a total of about 27% to cover per labour additives like eight days sick pay entitlement, 10 paid public holidays, 5% compulsory employees' superannuation, compulsory workers' compensation insurance and four weeks leave, including a 17.5% holiday pay loading.

Additionally, if the total annual labour bill is likely to exceed $500,000, the state government will levy a payroll tax of around 7% of the annual gross wages (excluding superannuation and workers' compensation). As payroll tax assessment varies from one state to another, and from one state budget to the next, check up on up-to-date rules with an accountant in the relevant state.

Working Hours

Working hours depend on the nature of the business. In broad terms, most manufacturing industries, public corporations and service industries such as banks and insurance companies work a five-day week from Monday to Friday. For those paid by the week, the standard work week is 38 hours, not including meal breaks such as lunch, and morning and afternoon tea.

In the days when union power was greater, working outside the core hours of eight to five on weekdays attracted various penalty rates. In recent years, however, the trend has shifted to flexible working hours, particularly in retail. Hours worked over the standard work week are usually regarded as overtime hours and attract a rate of 1.5 times the basic labour rate or twice the labour rate, depending on the number and timing of hours worked.

In some industries, workers consider obtaining a prescribed amount of overtime an unstated right. Shift work penalties of 10% to 20% may still apply in some industries for employees working outside "normal" nine-to-five hours. For industries such as retail, working at all hours of the day and night without attracting penalties is now becoming a normal condition of employment.

Awards and Employment Contracts

Historically, the blue collar labour force worked under awards and the white collar labour force worked under individual contracts. Blue collar awards not only set the minimum pay rates for particular occupations, but also the terms of employment contracts between employer and employee. Examples of topics covered in awards were entitlements to sick leave, holidays and allowances (e.g. tool allowances), services provided by the employer (e.g. working clothes), safety equipment, and change room facilities. Awards may fall under federal legislature or under the legislature of individual states.

Awards specify the minimum rate of pay. Employees, particularly in skilled trades, have been paid over award rates (by about 25% in most cases) for many years, regardless of whether they are employed under award employment conditions or not.

Whether to use an award as a condition of employment is voluntary for both parties. Use of an award for first-time foreign investors offers the advantage of saving the investor the time and expense of preparing their own employment conditions. On the other hand, the conditions of awards are thought by some employers to be weighted too heavily in favour of the employee. In addition, some awards have degenerated into excessively long documents written in legalese.

The 1996 federal government set much political store in "freeing up the labour market". It brought in new federal laws that resembled the recent New Zealand legislation. The new laws removed some of the barriers to employment such as the unfair dismissal laws of the previous Labor government. These new laws made removing unsatisfactory staff easier.

Under the new labour arrangements, the government and industry groups support individual employment contracts between employer and employees. This fundamental change in the relationship between employer and employee has come as a shock to some, for instance, public servants. No longer do any real or implied lifetime employment arrangements exist. An increased level of insecurity is thought to have affected some markets, such as the housing market, where people are less inclined to sign long-term mortgage agreements because they no longer feel they have long-term jobs.

New labour legislation has also eroded the power of the unions. As is always the case, the legislation varies from one state to another. States with entrenched right wing regimes have legislated more actively against the rights of employees than others.

Western Australia's Labour Laws

In 1997, Western Australia passed labour laws that were so draconian they violated 25 provisions of the International Labour Organisation (ILO) regulations in regard to the freedom of assembly and the right to strike.

Labour Productivity

Labour productivity has increased, along with the other OECD countries that have become mature economies after a period of rebuilding following World War II.

In the 1990s, the annual productivity of Australian industry rose faster than the previous decade as various measures, such as tariff reductions and legislation for more workplace flexibility, made their impact on industry. Recent productivity trends worldwide suggest that the introduction of computers in the last decade may finally be producing a measurable effect on labour productivity. The average annual increase in productivity over the last 30 years has been about 2%.

Advertising and Marketing

Before 1996, advertising was regulated by the government through the Advertising Standards Council (ASC), which was responsible for advertising standards based on public taste and decency. The ASC had the power to have offensive advertising removed from public display. However, the Liberal government voted in at the 1996 election believed more strongly in self-regulation than its predecessor. The ASC was disbanded and replaced by a group appointed by the advertisers themselves, the Australian Advertisers National Association (AANA), under whose aegis advertising standards have become decidedly more liberal.

Marketing consultants with telemarketing services can help collect market information or direct sell the product. Business associations and ethnic networks can also supply marketing information. Most capital cities have exhibition buildings operating an almost continuous programme of trade shows.

For products sold to more specific markets, an ever-changing selection of specialist magazines is published in Australia, with advertising space available.

In addition, Australia has several national newspapers and most states have two or three local newspapers. There are three or four commercial TV channels in capital cities and 10 to 15 commercial radio channels. Use of the Internet is increasing.

Unsolicited direct mail (otherwise known as "junk mail") is prevalent in Australia. There are many companies that can assist in the production and distribution of brochures and leaflets.

Almost all businesses are listed in the *Yellow Pages*. Separate phone books cover each capital city and provincial area. A business would first list in the Yellow Pages for the geographical area in which it is situated. If a wider geographical coverage is required, a company can list in the Yellow Pages outside its area of business. The entry costs are based on the population of the telephone area covered by the particular phone book.

Banking
While the Reserve Bank of Australia (RBA) does not underwrite any bank or financial institution in the country, a popular belief is that the RBA would act as a lender of last resort should one of the major Australian banks face a serious run on its reserves. The RBA imposes certain minimum levels of liquidity on banks and monitors their performance. Under the Financial Corporations Act, financial institutions must regularly inform the RBA all the details of trading operations including assets, liabilities, borrowings, lending, investments, and interest rates paid and charged.

Banking in Australia is sophisticated and integrated with banking worldwide. Banks are open for business Monday to Friday from 9.30 am to 4.30 pm and provide a wide range of electronic services, the use of which they encourage to reduce banking costs.

However, 19th century banking practices are still prevalent in many areas. Most transactions are made with cheques. Many companies still pay their wages by cash, giving the weekly payroll details to a wages delivery service and receiving the pay packets courtesy of an armoured van.

The Persistence of the Pay Packet

An engineering shop in Brisbane decided that directly crediting pay to employees' bank accounts would be more economical and convenient than paying wages in cash. However, when the system was implemented, the employees objected.

As the finance director later explained to the managing director, the company had overlooked one vital issue. When the (almost entirely male) workforce received their pay-packets in cash, the common practice was to skim a little beer money "off the top" before handing the rest of the pay-packet to their wives for banking. When direct debiting was introduced, husbands realised that, for the first time, their wives would know how much they were actually making. After receiving deputations from its workforce, the company reinstituted its contract with the Armaguard company to deliver the wages in cash.

Insurance

Insurance may be taken out to safeguard your business. Suggested cover is outlined below:

Building Insurance

Building insurance against fire, storm, damage and burglary of the building premises may or may not be included in the lease. If not provided by the landlord, cover can be taken out by the tenant. Similar cover should be taken out for the physical contents of the building such as the plant, equipment and stocks of material owned by the company.

Workers Compensation Insurance

Workers compensation insurance is compulsory, with the premiums paid by the employer. Workers compensation insures employees against the cost of injuries suffered at the workplace, including the cost of medical treatment and rehabilitation, plus the wages foregone. The premium charged for workers' compensation varies with the type of industry and the claims record of the company. It will normally be in the range of 2–5% of payroll.

Public Liability Insurance

Public liability insurance protects the company against injuries sustained by people not on the company's payroll while on the company's premises. Cover is limited to the amount shown on the policy. Cover of $5–10 million per incident is normal. The premium for this insurance is a few hundred dollars per year.

Product Liability Insurance

Product liability insurance protects against claims from consequential damage to customers and others, should a fault in the company's goods or services cause damage. Australia is a fairly litigious society with substantial rights given to people with whom the business may have no obvious contact. For protection against the possibility of some very expensive claims, a certain minimum level of product insurance is advisable. Like public liability insurance, a small premium will secure substantial cover.

Other Insurance Policies

Other insurance policies worth considering are for consequential damage and interruption to business and "key man" insurance (where the business is protected financially if the individual who is the driving force of the business falls sick or dies).

Product Design Rules

Additional quality requirements can be imposed where goods are of an intrinsically hazardous nature. For example, electrical goods are required to comply with national standards, foodstuffs are required to comply with health department regulations and packaging containing foodstuffs must be uncontaminated.

It should be noted that most of the laws covering quality and performance of goods are state laws, not federal laws. They are likely to vary between states. For example, cars have different regulations regarding collision safety features in each state .

The Australian Standards Association (ASA), a quasi-autonomous government organisation, is the principle authority in the country for setting the standards and specifications for goods and services. Australian standards used to be based on US and European standards. However, like most countries, over the past two or three decades, Australian has adopted standards issued by the International Standards Office (ISO).

Australia converted to the metric system of measurement in the late 1960s and early 1970s. The units of measurement in Australian standards and in industrial processes originating from the country are generally the Systeme International (SI) metric units, though some industries such as air conditioning suppliers still tend to work in imperial units. Due to the high level of imports from the United States, imperial hardware items are also widely available. Australians are accustomed to dealing with both the metric and imperial systems.

There is an increasing tendency for companies to become accredited with the Quality Standard ISO 9000 series of standards or their local equivalents. Companies not holding quality accreditation may find themselves excluded from an increasing number of markets, such as the auto industry and government contracts. Gaining ISO 9000 certification is an arduous and expensive business requiring considerable internal effort within the company and coordination with the accrediting authority. A minor industry of consultants in quality control exists to help client organisations establish Quality Control (QC) systems. Most companies seeking ISO 9000 certification engage quality consultants to prepare their documentation and train their staff.

Computers
Australia has enthusiastically embraced the computer age and has one of the world's highest rates of computer ownership and literacy.

In fact, it is becoming increasingly difficult to pass through the education system without access to computers. This means that increasing numbers of computer literate secondary school graduates enter the job market every year.

At the end of 1996, 47% of homes in the country had at least one personal computer, 15% had a modem and 7.4% of homes were connected to the Internet. There were 480 Internet Service Providers in the country. The rate of increase of Internet use is over 100% per year.

A vast range of computer software is available in Australia, both home-grown and made overseas (principally in the United States). For those buying off-the-shelf software, a general rule of thumb is to buy software written in Australia for commercial packages since it will incorporate Australian accounting and taxation rules. Technical software such as CAD/CAM packages and specialist design packages are generally written in their countries of origin for the international market.

Computers have become an indispensable tool of industry. In manufacturing, even small production runs are made using computer numerical control (CNC) equipment. Similarly, exotic methods of producing parts from the data files of designers—without an engineering drawing being used in the production sequence—are now becoming increasingly common.

Intellectual Property

Australia is an ideal place for investors looking for new ideas. Australians have an independent spirit and are innovative. Many dream of inventing a breakthrough product like the zip fastener that could make them rich beyond their wildest dreams. In this spirit, Australians generate patents at an impressive rate that is not in proportion to their population and have invented revolutionary products.

Patenting in Australia is handled by the Australian Intellectual Property Office (AIPO), which is affiliated to the World Intellectual Property Organisation (WIPO) of Geneva, Switzerland.

An inventor can protect his idea or product against copy by taking out a *provisional patent* or lodging a full *patent application*. The provisional patent is cheaper and gives the inventor the opportunity for the patent idea to be proven, prototyped and field tested. If the inventor takes out a provisional patent, a full patent application must be lodged at the end of 12 months. If the inventor fails to do so, not only does the patent idea lapse but it enters the public domain and can no longer be used as the basis for a future patent application.

Patent Applications

The fundamental requirement for granting a patent is that no one else should have thought of the idea. Patent applications on the wheel have been unsuccessful not because the wheel is covered by an existing patent, but because the wheel is no longer a new idea. The patent examiner must also be convinced that the patent idea will actually work. The yearly supply of patent applications for perpetual motion machines are never successful.

A trademark can be a word, picture, symbol or any combination of these. Once you register a trademark, you have the exclusive right to use it in Australia. A registerable trademark must be unique and distinctive, and if it is a word, it must not already be in use. You can refer to the trademark database to determine whether a trademark has already been registered.

Consumer Legislation

Consumer legislation is the responsibility of the states. While details of legislation vary from one state to another, the laws of all states have a common origin in British Law. Historically, the principle of *caveat emptor*[1]—"Let the buyer beware"—applied. Under this principle, once the buyer accepts the goods on offer, he also accepts their defects. Over the years, the law has been changed to impose greater obligations on the seller.

The first legislation departing from *caveat emptor* and enshrining the rights of consumers was the Sale of Goods Act. Under this act, the fundamental obligation on the supplier of the goods is that goods should be "of merchantable quality and fit for the purpose for which they are to be used". Merchantability and fitness for purpose are implied conditions of the sale contract between the buyer and seller of goods and services and cannot be waived by the seller writing his own conditions of sale. If the quality of goods sold is not satisfactory, the buyer is entitled to have the goods repaired or replaced with goods of satisfactory quality. The Sale of Goods Act was the start of legislation that has imposed greater obligations on the seller and granted further rights to the buyer over the years, helping to generate an increasingly litigious society. Other provisions regarding the sale of goods are contained in the Trade Practices Act.

It should be noted that the contract of sale exists between the buyer and seller, not the buyer and the manufacturer. If, for example, an importer sells defective goods that, to the best of his knowledge, were in perfect order, the importer is still responsible under the Sale of Goods Act for fixing the buyer's problems. The importer cannot escape from his contract with the buyer by referring the buyer directly to the manufacturer. If the importer feels so inclined, he must pursue his own remedies with the manufacturer in a separate issue.

Conditions of Sale—Warranty Terms

While consumer legislation cannot legally be over-written by exculpatory conditions of the seller, conditions of sale are well worth writing, in particular, to define the on-going terms of warranty. Even if these terms merely replicate those of existing consumer legislation, they serve as reference points for buyers and sellers to resolve differences regarding after-sales service.

Under legislation, sellers of goods are obliged to warrant goods sold against defects caused by faulty design or manufacture. The extent of the warranty is to repair or replace the goods at the seller's expense. *Fair wear and tear* is exempted.

For example, a seller would not be expected to warrant wearing parts such as brake linings and tyres that have reached the end of their working life through normal use. Neither is the seller expected to warrant goods that the buyer has subjected to abuse (or *abnormal use*, as more delicately phrased by the law). For those selling a fairly fixed range of products, it is worth identifying in the conditions of sale which parts and usage patterns are and are not covered by the seller's warranty

Under most circumstances, the buyer is obliged to meet the expense of transporting the goods to some point nominated by the seller for the repairs to be effected. Usually, this is the seller's place of business, though some sellers subcontract warranty work to third party agencies. In Australia, the cost of transport can be considerable and the obligation to transport defective goods is often a sore point with buyers.

Typical conditions of sale can be found on the back of invoices, probably the most appropriate place to print the conditions of sale since the conditions cannot then become detached from the fundamental record of the sale. Under taxation law and accounting practices, buyers are obliged to retain invoices for a number of years as evidence of the sales transaction.

Payment Terms

At the start of a trading relationship, most suppliers will expect cash on delivery, but once creditworthiness is established, most of the later transactions will be on credit. The commercial standard for collection of receivables is 30 days after the end of the month in which goods are delivered, meaning that payment can lag behind the delivery of goods by up to two months. Most suppliers allow this interpretation of 30 days to slide into the first week of the following month. For example, goods or services delivered in March would most likely be paid in the first week of May.

To open an account, the supplier will require the completion of an "Account Application Form" by the buyer. Some suppliers also request directors' guarantees, which can be held against the director's personal assets in the event of a failure to pay.

Settling Disputes

Most commercial court cases arise through a breach of contract by one of the contracting parties. Breach of contract is a civil action that must be pursued in a civil court. Legal costs can be heavy. In fact, any form of legal dispute in Australia is likely to cost a lot of money.

A small claims tribunal exists for the purpose of resolving claims of $5,000 or less. The claim is heard by an arbitrator, to whom each party presents his/her own evidence. No solicitors are involved in issues heard by the small claims tribunal and there are no court costs. The decisions of the arbitrator of the small claims tribunal are binding in law.

For claims greater than $5,000, the small claims tribunal can provide conciliation services, but if they want to avoid the courts, the parties to the disagreement must reach their own settlement.

If a dispute arises about a matter greater than $5,000 that cannot be resolved through negotiation, an objective assessment should be made whether to pursue the claim through the courts. The (sometimes unpalatable) best option for a potential claimant is to write off the amount of the claim and move on. If the case goes to court, whether a litigant wins or loses, the action will most likely cost money. On the other hand, the amount at issue may be substantial and going to court may be the only way claimants can obtain their rights.

How Much Is it Worth?

The court system in Australia is not an efficient way to settle commercial disputes. The legal system is expensive and time-consuming. One rule of thumb is that unless the amount can be collected by the small claims tribunal, it is hardly worth going to court to try and collect sums less than $20,000, factoring in legal costs and the probability that even seemingly clear-cut cases might be lost on some legal "technicality". On the average, you can expect to expend about one-third of your settlement in legal fees. In the *Barrack Case* of 1989, a famous insurance dispute arising from the entrepreneurial excesses of the 1980s, the plaintiff won a $66 million settlement, only to see $46 million absorbed in legal fees.

Appeals can be made to a higher court if the verdict is unsatisfactory. However, the higher the court in which the action is being heard, the greater is the hourly rates of legal representatives allowed to practise in it, and therefore, the higher the costs.

You can also engage the services of a "no win no fee" lawyer who charges no fees but receives an agreed percentage of the settlement figure. This is a growing area of the law, similar to the commission law that has operated for years in the United States.

The resources of litigants are also greatly magnified if the issue is one which offers the possibility of taking a class action. Once again, the system is similar to that operating in the United States. Individual litigants with the same complaint can join forces to mount a single legal case against the party being sued. This enables an individual with few resources to sue the largest and the most powerful in the community.

Class Action
In the early 1990s, about 30,000 impoverished Papua New Guinean (PNG) villagers successfully sued Ok Tedi Mining, a consortium of Australia's biggest company BHP, the PNG Government and other minority shareholders. At issue was the effect on habitat of dumping mining waste into the PNG river system. The villagers initially claimed five billion dollars in damages. This case, run by the Australian legal firm Slater and Gordon, combined the elements both of a class action and "no win no fee" law. The solicitors acting for all of the 30,000 villagers charged no fees during the years that the case ran but when it was successfully concluded, they took a percentage of the multimillion dollar compensation package that was eventually negotiated. The case never went to court.

What You See Is What You Get

Like life itself, business relationships in Australia tend to be what they appear.

For the most part, people intend to carry out the commitments they make and information provided can generally be relied upon. If people do not have the information you want, they will normally tell you so. Most Australians will not claim they know something if they do not. Australians recognise the complexity of the world and that one person cannot know everything or even a small proportion of everything. If you are the boss, you will not lose face with your staff if you ask their advice. If you need expertise not available in your own organisation, it can readily be hired. Australian business culture has produced an industry of consultants specialising in various disciplines who can be engaged to provide all the advice a business normally needs.

Australians tend to be "upfront" to the point of being brusque. Dealings with Australians have the minimum of hidden agendas. What you see is normally what you will get.

CHAPTER 7

Culture and Cultural Origins

First Settlement

Australia's original settlers, the Aborigines, were thought to have arrived on the Australian continent from Asia sometime during the last Ice Age when sea levels were much lower than today. Opinions are split on the timing of the first arrivals. Estimates range from 160,000 years to 50,000 years ago. The estimated Aboriginal population at European settlement also varies widely—from about 250,000 to 3,000,000.

Aborigines were nomadic hunter-gatherers. They left very little physical evidence from which modern historians can recreate an image of their society.

Despite their pre-stone age culture, Aborigines developed a symbiotic relationship with the land. They understood that survival depended on preserving the biosphere in which they lived. They imbued the scarce resources of earth and water with a religious significance that persists today. Aborigines managed to live off the fragile Australian environment for at least 50,000 years, whereas 200 years of European settlement have been immensely damaging. Much of the present day conflict between Aborigines and descendants of European settlers stems from the pressures on the environment imposed by modern society.

European Contact

By the start of the 17th century, European sailors had made various landfalls on the northern coastline of the continent. In 1640, Abel Tasman, a Dutchman from Batavia in the East Indies, sailed down the entire length of the east coast to the island state of Tasmania , which he named Van Dieman's Land after the governor of Batavia who sponsored his voyage. The name of the island was changed to Tasmania a century or so later.

In 1770, the British Naval Lieutenant James Cook (later Captain), sailing an extensive exploratory voyage in the *Endeavour,* "took possession" of much of the east coast of Australia on behalf of King George III.

In 1776, the British lost the American colonies which had hitherto been their dumping ground for unwanted domestic convicts. British jails of the era became crammed beyond their capacity. The great European rivals of the British, the French, were also beginning to acquire interests in the Pacific. To head off the French and to solve the convict problem, the British established a permanent presence on the eastern shores of the Australian continent. The *First Fleet,* with 1030 convicts and their keepers, set sail from Portsmouth in southern England on 13 May 1787. The settlers landed at Sydney Cove on 18 January 1788 and founded the penal colony of New South Wales on behalf of the Crown.

Population Growth

The policy to populate the vast continent developed at an early stage. In the early part of the 19th century, small settlements were scattered along the coastline. The Europeans perceived that there were miles of empty space not only between settlements but also in the unexplored centre of the country. Initially, the British were concerned that rival colonial European powers might establish settlements of their own on the continent. Later, the "yellow peril" phobia developed—the fear that the teeming hordes from Asia might descend upon the unoccupied continent.

In 1831, the British Government started a scheme of assisted migration to boost the Australian population. Most of the migrants came from Britain and Ireland as free settlers, attracted by the prospect of a better life "down under". The character of the Australian colonies was slowly changing from a penal settlement into a country of opportunity. The last convict was transported to Australia in 1868.

In the 1850s, Australia developed a new appeal for migrants. Gold was discovered first in New South Wales and shortly afterwards in Victoria. Many groups of people participated in the 1850s gold rush. There was a particularly large influx of Chinese to the Victorian goldfields, plus "forty-niners" moving off the exhausted goldfields of California in 1849.

By the second half of the 18th century, all sectors of the Australian economy were booming, particularly wool. Lured by the opportunities in the promised land "down under", the rate of migration increased.

At the time of federation in 1901, the population had reached 3.8 million and the "yellow peril" phobia was in full swing. One of the first acts of the new federal government was to implement the now infamous White Australia Policy, the objective of which was to keep the Chinese out of Australia. At the same time, immigration from Europe was actively encouraged.

The prime minister in 1920, W. H. (Billy) Hughes, expressed the sentiment of the age: "Population is the golden key which will unlock all doors and sweep aside all obstacles." Hughes was talking exclusively about European migration. His was the dictum of "populate or perish", the offspring of "yellow peril".

Government-sponsored immigration continued throughout the first half of the 20th century. Until World War II, most immigrants were British or Irish, with the remainder mainly German or Scandinavian.

War was declared in Europe and later in the Pacific. Australian military forces served in both theatres. From an Australian perspective, the main event of the war was the advance of the Japanese forces through the West Pacific Islands. One by one, the dominoes fell—Malaysia, Singapore, the Indonesian Archipelago, the Philippines, the Solomon Islands and New Guinea. In New

Populate or Perish

The premise of "populate or perish" was that unless the country was populated, Asians would invade Australia despite any restrictive immigration laws[1] it chooses to write. The objective of the immigration policy was to people the country with suitable Europeans. Prospective immigrants to Australia were screened in their country of origin according to the eligibility criteria of the immigration department. The tests to screen out unwanted immigrants were a little more subtle than merely an investigation of their ethnic origins.

Australia not only wanted correct ethnicity but also good physical specimens of good character to serve as its future breeding stock. Qualifying procedures were designed to deselect the undesirables without necessarily identifying the reason for rejection. In this vein, the eligibility criteria included the European Language Test whereby the prospective immigrant was tested for fluency in any European language—including those spoken only by a small percentage of Europeans, such as Welsh or Flemish. The language chosen was at the discretion of the examining officer so that those already identified as unsuitable immigrants will be eliminated at this stage.

Guinea, however, the Japanese advance was halted. After New Guinea, the next stop would have been Australia.

After the war, there was no reason to halt either the White Australia Policy or European migration. The Japanese advance merely proved that the "yellow peril" theory was well founded. In 1947, the Commonwealth signed an agreement with the International Refuge Organisation to resettle Europeans whom the war had displaced. By 1952, the displaced Europeans resettled in Australia numbered 170,000.

The White Australia Policy was abandoned in the early 1970s but the immigration programme continued. Migrants were no longer restricted on the grounds of race, though quotas were and still are placed on the overall level of migration.

White Australia
In 1948, the Labor Party Minister of Immigration, Arthur Calwell, coined the term *New Australians* to replace the term *Migrants*, which had acquired negative connotations in the community. Calwell is perhaps now better remembered for an infamous comment in support of White Australia—"Two Wongs do not make a white".

The source of migrants has become more dispersed in recent years and less focused on Europe.

Source of Migrants (1995–1996)

Country	Number of Migrants
New Zealand	12,265
Britain	11,268
China	11,247
Hong Kong	4,361
India	3,700
Vietnam	3,567
Bosnia	3,405
Philippines	3,232
South Africa	3,190
Former Yugoslavia	3,049

With the rise of environmental consciousness in the community, "populate or perish" has lost some of its advocacy. Some in the community now hold an opposite view that might be broadly stated as "populate *and* perish". These are people who are concerned about dwindling environmental resources and consider that the population of the country already exceeds its long-term sustainable carrying capacity.

The Aborigines

Of the total Australian population in 1996, 1.3% are classified as Aborigines and 0.1% are Torres Strait Islanders[2]—people who had the entire Australian continent to themselves for 50,000 years.

European settlement entirely disrupted Aboriginal culture. The penal settlement of the *First Fleet* was formed under conditions of incredible hardship and brutality inflicted on convicts and Aborigines alike. The British in Australia made no attempt to understand Aboriginal culture and saw Aborigines as mere obstructions to development.

"Ethnic Cleansing" in the 19th Century

In the 19th century, the Tasmanian Government organised a bizarre manhunt, where a line of settlers walked the entire length of the island with the intention of corralling the Aboriginal population onto a southern headland where they could be rounded up and shipped to a "safe location".

The chosen destination was King Island, a small unpopulated island in the Bass Strait. After walking for a month, they realised they had captured almost no one—only a woman and two children found sleeping under a log. The rest of the Aboriginal population had slipped, unnoticed, through the settlers' line.

After the unsuccessful roundup, the ethnic cleansing of Tasmania resumed. Gradually, the Aboriginal population of Tasmania was totally eradicated—to the last man, woman and child. The last of them died in 1876.

At the end of the 19th century, the mainland Aboriginal population had dwindled. The Aborigines who remained had few rights. The Founding Fathers ducked the Aboriginal issue in writing the constitution. Instead of incorporating Aboriginal rights into the constitution, the Founding Fathers passed the responsibility for Aboriginal affairs to the states. Granting citizenship rights to

Aboriginal Land and the Lost Generation

The mere passing of time has not settled the controversial issue of squatters' rights to land they occupied in the 19th century. Two high court judgements, the 1993 *Mabo* decision and the 1997 *Wik* decision, found that leases granted under duress by the Crown to the squatters generations before still entitled the Aboriginal tribes to occupy land that the pastoralists had grazed for four or five generations.

The pastoralists' response to this has been to lobby the government to change the law so that native title will be "extinguished". The native title issue has created a great deal of heat in the community. Human rights groups elsewhere in the world have become interested. If the extinguishment option is adopted by the federal government, Aboriginal spokespeople will have raised the possibility (amongst others) of approaching black African nations to boycott the 2000 Sydney Olympic Games.

In 1997, the government-sponsored Lost Generation Enquiry found that, until 1970, Aboriginal children had been forcibly separated from their parents. The ostensible purpose of this practice was to give the Aboriginal children a "better life" by raising them in a white environment. The children grew up in orphanages or with white foster parents without knowing who their real families were. In 1997, after details were made public, Aboriginal leaders requested that Prime Minister John Howard officially apologise on behalf of the government for the indignities inflicted on the "lost generation" of children.

When the PM demurred, Aborigines took out a full page open letter in *The Times* of London, stating their position two days before Howard, on a state visit to the United Kingdom, was scheduled to meet Queen Elizabeth II.

the Aborigines took the states almost 50 years and it was finally completed in 1967.

Aborigines and Torres Strait Islanders are the only ethnic group in Australia for whom separate laws are made. The objective of the separate laws is to help them as a disadvantaged group rather than to disadvantage them further. They receive special benefits in education, housing and social welfare.

No Aborigine has headed a commercial enterprise of any significance. However, there have been a number of politically active Aborigines in public life and their numbers are increasing rapidly, as Aborigines acquire more educational opportunities and confidence in their public voice.

Probably the highest political office attained by an Aborigine was that of Pastor Doug Nicholls, who was governor of South Australia between 1976 and 1977. Nicholls had previously been a famous boxer, football player and Aboriginal political activist.

Entering the 21st century, the growing political power of the Aborigines is affecting the country's economy. The highest court of law in the country has confirmed that Aborigines hold legally enforceable land rights over much land that miners and agriculturists want to utilise for other purposes.

The Aborigines have acquired eloquent and educated spokespeople, mostly qualified lawyers, who understand the points at which pressure can be exerted on the Australian Government to advance Aboriginal causes. In particular, interracial issues of historical origin can be played out in global public arenas under the scrutiny of the world media.

Multiculturalism

In many ways, Australia is still a nation of immigrants. Twenty-two percent of people living in Australia were born in another country. The figures for other high immigrant countries, such as the United States and Canada, are 9% and 13% percent respectively. The immigration rate is even higher in the major cities—37% of Sydney residents were born outside Australia.

The Australian Government's official policy in this area is *multiculturalism*, under which people are encouraged to maintain the cultural identity of their originating societies while harmonising with other communities. Multiculturalism has been one of the outstanding success stories of Australian society. In Australia, minority groups import their own culture, which they are free to practice in the country.

Contrary to some recent images, Australia is an exceptionally tolerant society with little racial disharmony. Different ethnic groups exist in most major populations centres, into which new arrivals can integrate. The government is conscious of the ethnic mix and legislates against racism. In fact, it was seriously suggested that the Anti-Racism Act be extended to declare the telling of a racist joke a civil offence. This proposed amendment was abandoned due to the complications in enforcing it.

Ethnicity* (1987 figures)

Anglo Celtic	74.5%
North West European	7.4%
Southern European	7.4%
Eastern European	3.9%
West Asian (includes Middle. East)	2.1%
Other Asian (China, Japan)	1.5%
Southeast Asian	1.2%
Aboriginal	1.0%
South Asian	0.6%

* Ethnicity is defined as "ethnic strength"—aggregate percentage of the ethnicity by the proportion of each group of the parentage of each individual

The Positives

Australians like to experience the lifestyles of different cultural groups inside and outside their own country. Outside the school yard, Australian society presents few serious inter-tribal conflicts. Excitable minority groups occasionally exercise their traditional rivalries through peaceful demonstrations at which egg-throwing is the extreme expression of violence. Bloodshed is rare. Laid-back mainstream Australia provides a matrix in which the rival ethnic groups can peacefully coexist. Australians are a racially tolerant, easy-going society where everyone is entitled to do his or her own thing—within reason, of course. People are free to choose their own customs and religions, provided they do so within the laws of the host country. Being an immigrant is not a barrier to personal progress. A person's status is determined more by his or her own efforts than breeding or ethnicity.

In Australia, cultural subgroups tend to congregate. For example, Melbourne has the largest Greek population outside Athens, many of whom live in a cluster of suburbs north of the city centre.

Specific groups of immigrants tend to be attracted to certain occupations. Italians, for example, have become the leading subcontractors for concreting and road works. At the pinnacle of this industry are companies like Grollo Brothers—the country's biggest high-rise construction company—and Transfield, the country's biggest heavy civil engineering company. Both were formed by first generation Italian families who made good.

The Jews, who make up only 1% of the Australian population, have been extremely successful in the financial sector. In fact, the Jews make up 25% of the annual *Business Review Weekly's* "rich list".[3]

Every major city has its Chinatown and the Vietnamese buy up entire shopping streets in chosen suburbs.

Restaurants from every imaginable country can be found in the major cities. If you enjoy Asian food, you will find that it is easy enough to find an Asian restaurant. The toughest problem is finding one that has not westernised the Asian taste to the point of blandness—despite the fact that virtually all Asian restaurants are run by Asians. Perhaps the best Asian restaurants are those at the bottom end of the market with a clientele made up of Asian students. Australian cities probably have the widest range of

One of the many Vietnamese stores along Springvale Road in Melbourne.

foodstuffs for sale in the world, with specialist supermarkets selling food to suit all palates.

There are local and foreign language newspapers in all the major tongues—Italian, Greek, Chinese and Vietnamese. Major cities also have radio stations in languages like Italian and Chinese. The government-run ethnic television station, SBS, broadcasts in all major cities and is entirely devoted to ethnic programmes produced in the originating countries.

The Negatives

On the down side, unemployment is persistently higher among recent immigrants. Even highly-qualified people trained in the engineering and medical fields have to settle for jobs as security guards or bellhops while they seek more qualified work.

Women, in particular, tend to feel discriminated against in the workforce. In fact, migrant women is the group with the highest rate of unemployment. Professional working women will find that it is extremely difficult to engage a maid to mind children during working hours. Asked why they come to Australia where they may find life more difficult than in their country of origin, many women state that they think that Australia is a land of opportunity or that they have migrated to give their children a better quality of life.

Quite often, foreign educational qualifications are not recognised. Holders of seemingly adequate foreign qualifications, such as medicine, may have to be re-examined at Australian institutions in order to practice their professions in the country. Australia has a Central Qualifying Board to assist migrants upgrade their qualifications.

Religion

Christianity, with its various sects, is the dominant religion in Australia. According to the 1996 population census, 70% of Australians professed to believe in the afterlife. Despite this, religion does not have a strong foothold in Australia. Attendances at religious ceremonies have been falling for years.

Australians are tolerant of all religions. Muslims living in Australia may practise their religion with the same passion they do everywhere else. No religion is banned unless it seriously disrupts civil order. Generally speaking, the issue of religion does not arise in everyday life. In fact, religion is a subject one does not normally enquire about when meeting another person for the first time. Other taboo topics include a person's political inclinations, age and salary.

Religion is not normally a part of business negotiations unless it gives you access to a particular group. Exceptions occur in ethnic minorities. For instance, Judaism and business are interrelated to some extent.

Australian English

Not understanding English is a severe disadvantage for immigrants. Although other languages are spoken between migrants, in migrant homes and within the ethnic media, Australia is essentially a monolingual, English-speaking country.

Generally, Anglo-Saxon Australians lack a good "ear" for foreign languages. Many Australians expect people to learn their own language without making a serious attempt to learn anyone else's, even when they travel abroad. Australian English speakers are not especially tolerant of those speaking foreign tongues. If they do not understood, they will tend to repeat the message louder rather than slower. In fact, many Australians are fairly inarticulate in the one language they do speak. Australian public speakers, as well as the average citizen, express themselves less ably than their counterparts in other English-speaking countries like Britain and the United States. Australian politicians are notorious for poor public speaking.

Sir Joh

Perhaps the least articulate Australian public speaker of the 20th century is Sir Johannes Bjelke-Petersen, the premier of Queensland between 1968 and 1987. Sir Joh's mangling of the language was legendary. In fact, his use of the language was so unconventional that he practically invented his own dialect and became the favourite subject of impersonators at that time.

In 1987, Sir Joh initiated a bizarre political campaign for the office of prime minister. As the then foreign minister, Bill Hayden, observed in federal parliament: "Had the campaign been successful, and had Joh in his capacity as prime minister had cause one day to address the United Nations, he would have been the only English-speaking delegate in the history of that assembly for whom a translator would have been required."

Australian English can be difficult for people from other English-speaking countries to understand. To other English speakers, the Australian vernacular stretches and flattens vowels to the breaking point while consonants are truncated. This gives the language a monotonic quality, where the separation of words is difficult to distinguish.

"Owyergoinorright?"

The legendary Australian greeting, "Owyergoinorright?"—uttered as a single word without internal intonation—if written down, would read, "How are you going, all right?" (a translation which might convey little additional information to a foreigner anyway). Other single-word phrases that strain the foreign ear include "aorta" meaning "they ought to" (an appeal to the ubiquitous forces of authority), "eggnitioning" meaning air-conditioning and "airfridge" meaning average.

The impact of the dialect on a newly-arrived Italian migrant was the subject of John O'Grady's best selling comic novel of the 1950s, *They're a Weird Mob*—a book that is still worth reading today.

Australian accents vary somewhat between socioeconomic groups and between states. Country accents and the accents of blue collar workers are broader and flatter than city accents and the accents of white collar workers. To a foreigner, a Sydney barrister will be much easier to understand than a rural worker in Northern Queensland. A form of "posh" Australian, spoken with upper class English intonation, exists in some sections of the socialite groups and the legal fraternity. However, this form of Australian English is not particularly widespread and is thought by many to be an affectation.

Elections and the Media

The spin that the media puts on the news greatly shapes the views of the community. This is particularly apparent at election time.

In Australia, as in other democracies, policy differences between opposing parties have narrowed in recent years. Election outcomes are based less on policies and more on the personality and presentation of the party leaders. Virtually every Australian has a television set, through which leaders of political parties can join one in a fireside chat around election time. While ostensibly voting for their local Member of Parliament, in many cases, Australians may not actually know who their local members are. They vote for the leader they like the most. Or, if they are cynics, they vote for the one they dislike the least.

A healthy democracy is one in which opposing viewpoints are presented in equal measure. With the intention of ensuring that the media maintains diversity of viewpoint, the Australian Government has legislated the Cross Media Ownership Laws restricting how much of the media (newspapers and television stations) a single media proprietor could own in each city. In recent years, powerful media proprietors have influenced weak governments to compromise the good intentions of these laws.

The number of newspapers in Australia has declined over the years as the readership starts to receive its news in other forms, mainly television. Today, there are two morning papers in the largest cities and one in the smaller cities. There is also a national newspaper (*The Australian*) and a national financial newspaper (*The Australian Financial Review*). In addition, a large number of general and specialist magazines and periodicals, as well as imported copies of foreign newspapers, are also available from news agencies in the major cities. Australian-published foreign language newspapers with circulations of up to 20,000 have also been on sale for over 70 years.

The relationship between the press and politicians in Australia has been fractious at times. Commonly, neither side affords much courtesy to the other. Journalists often insult the politicians with loaded questions and politicians respond with questions of their own regarding the interviewer's credentials, their salary and their rights to employment or to life itself. Often, interviews produce far more acrimony than information. Politicians seem to be at particular loggerheads with the Australian Broadcasting Corporation (ABC), which is the government-owned TV and radio broadcasting network that is traditionally critical of whichever party is in power.

Tall Poppies and Political Culture

There are those in Australia who talk about the "tall poppy syndrome". This phrase describes a mental condition, whether real or imagined, that while most Australians admire their heroic role models, they also do not mind seeing them cut down to size every now and then.

It must be said that those Australians who criticise other Australians for their tall poppy syndrome usually see themselves as tall poppies who, naturally enough, wish to remain that way.

The tall poppy syndrome may or may not be true. Australians rarely put down their Nobel Prizewinning scientists, their inventors and innovators or their outstanding literary figures.

The tall poppies Australians tend to attack are the *nouveau riche* who often acquire their new-found wealth under dubious circumstances. The entrepreneurs of the 1980s were an entire group of tall poppies who were later cropped to public satisfaction.

The tallest poppy of his day, Alan Bond, became a bankrupt and went to jail.[4] Perhaps there are those in the community, suffering the tall poppy syndrome, who delighted in the fall of Alan Bond. Then again, the financial damage that Bond wrought was spread widely across the community.

The flip side of tall poppy is mediocrity. If Australians are so consumed by jealousy that they yearn to see their high achievers fail, do they feel more comfortable having mediocre leaders, people who are more like them, people of modest talents and achievements?

Political Role Models

In this regard, some of the politicians that Australia has produced are particularly interesting. Under the Australian political system, all that disqualifies a candidate from standing for political office is a criminal record or a mental condition. No academic qualifications or track record of achievement are necessary. No psychological aptitude or intelligence tests are conducted. In fact, there are no particular selection criteria at all.

The Member for Oxley

In the 1996 election, an independent, Pauline Hanson, won the seat of Oxley in Queensland. Shortly after her elections, Pauline Hanson became the most well-known first-term politician in the country. This was because, in her maiden speech, Pauline Hanson spoke on the subject, "Yellow Peril Revisited", spiced up by some Aboriginal bashing.

The speech and its aftermath created mayhem in the local media and in nearby countries. Painting her own picture of Asia, Pauline Hanson's speech was peppered with many elementary factual errors presented as exaggerated threats, for instance, she claimed that the population of Malaysia was 200 million when it was less than 20 million. Pauline Hanson, it seemed, merely made up facts to fit her prejudices.

In 1997, Pauline Hanson formed her own political party—somewhat ambiguously called the One Nation Party. Pauline Hanson then developed pretensions of becoming the Australian prime minister after the One Nation Party sweeps to victory in the next election.

Prior to becoming a parliamentarian, Pauline Hanson was a bar maid and the proprietor of a fish and chip shop. Despite her lack of qualifications, she beat all the other candidates at the Liberal Party pre-selection ballot for the seat. Not all Australian politicians, however, are as completely unqualified as Pauline Hanson. About half the politicians in Australia are lawyers. Others are qualified in other fields.

However, unqualified people have played dominant roles in Australian politics. Many Australians prefer leaders with a large dose of "average bloke" qualities. Even the highly qualified Australian politicians come with large slabs of "blokesiness". Australia has shown a propensity to elect and, more importantly, *re-elect* leaders who have—in the Australian vernacular—a "larrikin" streak. Australians seem to enjoy the spectacle of their leaders breaking laws that they themselves created.

Just Another Bloke on the Block...

In 1995, the Liberal Party leader Dr. John Hewson—with a PhD in economics, film star good looks, style and a charismatic personality—was replaced by John Howard, an ex-suburban solicitor and a Mr. Magoo look-alike, whose election platform expressed strong support for family values and "Aussie Battlers".

Bob Hawke, Australia's most re-elected prime minister, was noted for his drinking exploits. He once had an entry in the Guinness Book of Records as the fastest man in history to drink a yard of ale.

Sir Joh Bjelke-Petersen, Queensland's longest-serving premier, was noted for his cavalier treatment of the press—whom he disdained—and his reference to the process of issuing statements at press conferences as "feeding the chooks".[5] During his term, the parliament in Queensland broke all records for the least number of sitting days. Bjelke-Petersen ruled by issuing decrees from his living room.

Paul Keating, the prime minister from 1991 to 1996, was nicknamed the "Lizard of Oz" by the British Press because of his disregard for stiff upper lip protocol in a meeting with the Queen. Keating was the protagonist in a parliament that dropped language standards to a new low. Some of Keating's more memorable descriptions of honourable members on the opposition benches were "scumbags" and "dogs returning to their vomit". While he was treasurer, Keating's excuse for failing to file his own tax return by the stipulated time was that he was too busy running the financial affairs of the nation.

Other Role Models
Few Australian role models are urbane and sophisticated. Probably the most popular comedian in the country in the last 30 years is Barry Humphries, who is perhaps more widely known by his alter egos, Dame Edna Everage and Sir Les Patterson. As Dame Edna, Barry Humphries mercilessly satirises the Australian suburban housewife of the 1960s, and as the uncouth drunkard, Sir Les Patterson, he satirises the country's politicians.

Paul Hogan, the actor who made it big in Hollywood, is another popular comic whose shows gently satirise community issues from a working class perspective.

Various sporting celebrities are admired for their brawn rather than their brain or their style. Favoured Australian stereotypes, the "Rough Diamond" and the "Aussie Battler", flow from the archetypal pioneering stock of the last century.

Regional Rivalries
One hundred years after federation, colonial traditions live on as interstate rivalry. This is usually not a very serious affair, conducted more on the sporting field than elsewhere. Interstate rivalry is exercised, in particular, between the two largest cities, Sydney and Melbourne.

Of "Bananabenders", "Sandgropers" and "Croweaters"…
States disparage their rivals with mildly derogatory nicknames. Queenslanders are known as "bananabenders", West Australians as "sandgropers", South Australians as "croweaters", Victorians as "bullants" and Tasmanians as the not very imaginative "taswegians". At the same time, Tasmanians refer to Australians from all the northern states as "mainlanders".

Visitors to Australia may be puzzled about some Australians' reference to "the country". People may tell you that they come from "the country" or "the bush" although you know that they live in Bendigo or Dubbo—cities with populations of over 25,000—and work in a factory. In this context, coming from "the country" or "the bush" just means not living in one of the capital cities—it does not indicate a rural lifestyle or occupation. The other half of the population that does not live in "the bush" lives in "the city", which is a mildly censorial term for any of the six state capitals and the federal capital. Bush dwellers still affiliate themselves with the pioneering images of the past.

Civic pride is prominent in the bush. Country towns and cities are close-knit communities. People in tropical outback Queensland, for example, like to think of themselves as "Northern Queenslanders" (a greatly superior species) rather than merely "Queenslanders". Northern Queenslanders of this mindset regard anyone living south of the Tropic of Capricorn in the vast expanse of Southern Queensland to be a "city slicker".

Australians often express pride in their origins as if they controlled the genetic accident that was their own birth. Those holding this view of the world will often add words like "and proud of it" when they explain that they were born in (and have never left) some microscopic and forgettable townlet somewhere beyond the "Back of Bourke".[6]

Tasmania is the smallest and most economically disadvantaged state in the Commonwealth and can sometimes inadvertently be ignored—a slip that Taswegians are extremely sensitive about. At one Commonwealth Games, Tasmania was omitted from the map of Australia—the island having apparently sunk beneath the surface of the Southern Ocean. Cries of Taswegian outrage could be heard clear across the Bass Strait.

Visitors to Tasmania should take care not to say that they have flown in "from Australia" when they have in fact merely moved from one part of Australia to another. If, for instance, you have just flown from Melbourne to Hobart, you have not just arrived "from Australia", you have just arrived "from the mainland".

Incorrect terminology in this area would almost certainly jeopardise a visitor's putative business dealings.

Australia's Relations with the World

For some decades, the brash and outgoing attitude that Australians projected to the outside world seemed to have been moderated by hesitancy in recent years as the country reassesses its role in the world order. Australians of recent years have tended to stand somewhat in thrall of the economic activities of the Asian Tigers, though with the recent implosion of the Asian economies, this perception is changing once again.

This period of introspection may explain some of the images the country has in recent times projected overseas. During its "yellow peril" days, Australia feared Asian invasion. The current fear is Asian economic domination. The more Australian golf courses are developed by the Japanese (who have not got too many in their own country), the more people worry that the country is being "sold out". The fact is that Australia is a vast country with no shortage of land. Only about 3% of Australian real estate is owned by foreigners.

Nonetheless, some Australians feel that they are losing control of their own destiny—that they are being "taken over". That the colony is itself being "colonised". As a result, a small minority of the country (perhaps 5%) has sympathised with Pauline Hanson's simplistic views that the best course of action is to raise the drawbridge and withdraw from the rest of the world. People such as Hanson and, to some extent, John Howard, would like to retreat to the safety of the past, into the Fortress Australia they used to occupy at a time when they appeared to be their own masters.

However, this is a view that cannot be reconciled with the realities of the present and the projections for the future. Globalisation appears to be an unstoppable force. Today's citizens of Northern Queensland are likely to give birth to tomorrow's citizens of the world, along with attendant responsibilities for issues that cannot be contained within national borders: technological development, food shortages, disease control and deterioration of the environment.

CHAPTER 8

Culture at the Personal Level

Multicultural Overview

Multiculturalism is an official government policy in Australia, where people have become accustomed to living in close proximity with other nationalities. People of different cultures coexist harmoniously, with the Anglo-Saxon group making up the predominant culture.

Australians are casual and relaxed about protocol. Visitors do not have to bend over backwards to adopt the host culture. In any case, the chances are that Australians may find your culture more fascinating than their own.

If you are a stranger to Australia and in doubt about how to behave, do whatever is appropriate in Great Britain or North America and you will almost certainly not offend anyone.

Body Language

Australian standard body language is similar to British practice. Touching between heterosexual men is minimal. Men shake hands on meeting, departing, making wagers and congratulating each other. Handshaking is performed with the right hand. The handshake is firm. A weak handshake is thought to indicate a weak character. On the other hand, a bone-crushing handshake is anti-social. The correct attitude of the hand is with the palm perpendicular to the ground. Turning the hand 90 degrees with a downward palm is an aggressive stance. A double-handed handshake is unusual. Putting an arm around the shoulders of another man is not normal practice unless he is a particularly close friend or is physically handicapped and in need of help.

Women to women body language is less structured. Women meeting in business are most likely to shake hands the same way as men. Women friends reuniting shake hands, hug and kiss, depending on their moods.

Man to woman body language varies with the degree of intimacy of the relationship. When meeting for the first time, men and women may shake hands or merely wave to each other at close range.

Personal space around Australians tends to be greater than most cultures—two feet is a good working rule. When two people are engaged in a conversation, they will normally maintain strong eye contact. Looking away is thought to indicate lack of confidence or insincerity. Appropriate hand gestures, shoulder shrugging, head nodding and shaking are aids to conversation. As in most places, pointing with the index finger is aggressive. A thumbs up gesture indicates agreement while a finger up gesture either with one or two fingers is an insult.

Courtesy and Customs

Despite the advent of equal opportunity between sexes, courtesies are still extended to women. Men usually (but not always) open doors for women, help them in and out of chairs and allow them to walk ahead. The practice of standing up when a new guest joins a dinner party is becoming less common—so is opening and shutting car doors for women. The phenomenon of men footing the bill is certainly less common now that most women are in the workforce and may earn as much or even more than men.

The Home

When Australians entertain guests in their homes, women generally do the bulk of the food preparation although men tend to take charge of the barbecuing. It is a good idea to bring something to the party, such as a bottle of drink, some titbits, a present for the children, or all three.

It is normal, though not expected, that guests help with menial tasks like shuttling food and beverages around the party, and

The home is very important to Australians. The country has one of the highest rates of home-ownership in the world.

perhaps washing the dishes. Australians rarely have domestic help or waiter service, although the occasional party is catered.

Home entertainments are often buffet affairs where guests help themselves to cutlery and crockery. At more formal dinners, the guest may be greeted by a bewildering array of cutlery. The normal practice, if unsure of what piece of cutlery to use, is to watch an adjacent diner. If this fails, work from the outside of the arrangement for the first dish to the inside for the last.

The home, as represented by the actual structure itself, is an important status symbol and psychological prop. Home ownership in Australia has long been an important tradition, although this has recently come under scrutiny.

An alternative view—peddled by yuppies and those associated with the stock market—that has recently come into vogue is that you could do better investing in stocks and shares than real estate. Therefore, renting makes more economic sense than buying.

Despite the attractions of the stock exchange, Australians have one of the highest rates of home ownership in the world. The home is likely to be the most important purchase that the average person ever makes. Regarded not merely as a place to live, but also as an investment, an Australian home is forever in the process of being extended and renovated.

The adjunct to the home is the garden, which is another object of absorbing interest. Australian gardens are generally modelled on English-style lawns and European flowers that can only survive the Australian climate by using prodigious amounts of water—the country's scarcest resource.

When Australians invite you to their homes, though it is probably for the pleasure of your company, they may also be displaying a statement of their assets or their skills at redecorating, particularly if they take the trouble of giving you a detailed tour of the house. Any appreciative comments you make about the quality of the structure and the standard of the decorating will be highly valued.

Greetings

The traditional Australian greeting used to be "G'day" or "G'die" meaning "Good day". This has now been pretty much replaced by "How are you?" Some immigrants and visitors find this greeting annoying because they mistakenly interpret it as a literal enquiry into the state of their health.

"How Are You?"

As Mrs. T. G. of Vermont, a recent English immigrant, complained in her letter to an Australian newspaper: "They keep asking how I am. Do I have to detail the state of my health 20 times a day? It's as if everyone in the country thinks they are the beneficiary to my life insurance policy."

Mrs. T. G. was taking the greeting too literally. There are a number of correct responses to "How are you?". The simplest is "Fine, thank you", or if you feel particularly frisky and want to respond with a local flavour, you may be "As fit as a Mallee bull!". Very often you are "Never better".

Your reply must not indicate a lack of enthusiasm for the state of your health. If you merely declare yourself to be "Okay", eyebrows will be raised. And it is absolutely incorrect to indicate any health problem. You must not say that you are "Not too well" or describe any specific ailment—"Terrible, my lumbago's killing me." Even if your doctor has given you ten days to live, at the very least, you are "Fine".

The other broad approach is to ignore the question entirely and reply with a mutually cancelling "How are you?" of your own.

Food

From the early days of European settlement, Australia adopted a British-style diet. Meat and three vegetables boiled beyond submission was the predominant fare.

Australian dietary theory of the 1950s subscribed to a Lamarckian view that the power of the animal being eaten was conferred to the consumer. A real man's breakfast was at that time steak and eggs, rather than the Uncle Toby's Oats of the "iron men" of today.

In this vein, food companies invented the hot meat pie—the ingredients of which are minced uncommercial cuts from the slaughter room encased in fatty pastry, flavoured with preservatives and laced with tomato sauce. Meat pies served piping hot in paper bags (that double as spillage containers) are still a favourite fast food for spectators at sporting events.

Multiculturalism has brought Australian diet a long way since the 1950s. Australians now consume a wide range of foods, and it is very difficult to identify a unique Australian food. There are

The Way of the Elephant
During a recent international cricket match in Melbourne, a rather paunchy Australian businessman was entertaining a slender Indian guest, who happened to be a vegetarian. The businessman suggested that perhaps a pie would put some meat on the Indian's skinny bones. The Indian demurred. In the Indian's opinion, (verified by coaches at the Australian Institute of Sport), vegetable matter bulked up quite well into muscles. "After all," the Indian pointed out to his Australian host, "observe the elephant."

restaurants catering to almost all ethnic groups and only the most extreme dietary conventions are frowned upon.

Table Etiquette

Australians have not developed the rigid dining protocols of many other societies. Table etiquette in Australia is fairly flexible.

Home entertaining is popular in Australia where the hosts will invite you over to their house to meet their wife and children. A home-made meal is usually the central feature of these events, whether it be a barbecue or a formal meal.

If you are attending a sit-down dinner, there will normally be a little pre-dinner mingling where drinks and plates of finger food (termed "nibbles") will circulate. When the time arrives for dinner proper, your host or hostess will indicate the seating arrangement. As in other Western countries, the food for each course is served at the same time, rather than at random times during the dinner.

After the food is placed on the table, let someone else start eating first—preferably the host or hostess. Though religion has lost its popularity in Australia, it is possible that grace[2] may be said at the start of the meal. If this happens, look gratefully at the food on your plate and say "Amen" at the end of the recital however you might feel about Christianity. Another possible pre-dinner ritual is a toast to the reason for the gathering by the host. Most likely the toast will be made to you as the guest!

The basic Anglo-Saxon eating "irons" are knives, forks and spoons. However, in ethnic restaurants or when ethnic food is served at home, culinary equipment appropriate to the meal being catered, for instance, chopsticks, will most likely be supplied.

For the Chopsticks-Challenged

An ingenious Australian inventor once introduced a set of chopsticks with a design improvement on which he took out a patent. This was a leaf spring at the handle end of the chopsticks to keep the two chopsticks together and thereby make them easier to handle, particularly for novice chopstick operators. The inventor declared his intention to make a fortune by saturating the Chinese market with these items but they never caught on—in China or anywhere else.

At barbecue parties, cutlery may not be supplied and the meat may be served between two slices of bread or between two halves of a bread roll.

Where there is a common dish, use of personal cutlery is absolutely improper. The common dish normally comes with its own cutlery—perhaps a spoon, fork, tongs or ladle—with which to convey the food to the plate of each individual. This may also apply to staples like butter and sauce where cutlery such as a butter knife or spoon is provided with each common dish.

Dress

Australians have a reputation for being atrocious dressers. Casual clothes tend to be excessively casual and, in extreme cases, some men wear only very short shorts (known as "stubbies") with thongs as the optional footwear. The casual standards for female outfits are only slightly more comprehensive.

Standard western dress code applies in business. Men wear suits and ties, and the standard business suit is of a darker shade, with blue and grey being the most popular colours. The quality of the cut and material of the suit are also important. Businesswomen wear suits or dresses.

In warmer climates, particularly in Queensland and Western Australia, the more comfortable menswear for day-to-day business is an ensemble of shorts, shirt (long or short sleeved), tie and long white socks.

Minister in Shorts
Though you would not normally wear shorts to your first appointment with a cabinet minister, you might find male ministers themselves attired this way. The former premier of South Australia, Don Dunstan, created quite a stir one day when he showed up at a parliamentary sitting wearing pink shorts.

Smart casual dress for men is slacks and shirt of any style. Years ago, most Australian men used to wear hats to work, though a business hat nowadays is most unusual.

Fashion colours for women vary as determined by fashion houses. Women's dress is unrestricted outside the normal bounds of good taste. Bare or covered limbs are equally acceptable.

If you are invited to play golf, opt for a more conservative attire. At the very least, your golf shirt should be collared. If you are wearing a golf cap, you should remember to remove it when inside the clubhouse. In some golf clubs, men who forget to remove their headgear on entering the clubhouse will have to buy a round of drinks for everyone in the bar! Women, on the other hand, can keep their headgear intact wherever they go. A venue where a hat is almost mandatory for both sexes are the horse races-cum-social gatherings such as the Melbourne Cup festivities in spring.

Foreign visitors who wish to wear the traditional outfits of their originating cultures at social events should feel free to do so.

Business Culture

Socialising in Business

In the 1970s, long tax-deductible business lunches, usually accompanied by generous quantities of alcohol, were a common business practice. Soon after, in the 1980s, the government decided to regard tax-deductible dining as "rorting" since there was no way for the taxation office to distinguish a legitimate business lunch from an office party. The then government scrapped the tax-deductibility entitlement to business entertainment.

Present day business lunches are likely to be brief affairs at nearby cafes or in the boardroom itself, where sandwiches can be delivered. Alternatively, the business luncheon may be a large formal affair served in a splendid dining hall where businessmen gather to rub shoulders with their ilk.

Evening cocktail parties are also popular as a form of business entertainment and present opportunities to get your business card circulating. Major cities usually have a number of business clubs, some with very restricted membership, which exist for the purpose of business entertaining and are generally located in fine old buildings in the city.

Much business entertaining is also conducted at the business person's home. These events could range from casual pool barbecues to black tie dinner parties. When invited to someone's home, you are advised to first enquire about the dress code.

If you are dining out, you may well find yourself in familiar surroundings. Australians may well press you to choose a restaurant serving your national food.

Guests may also be invited to attend various sporting events such as cricket matches and horse races. These events would normally be viewed in comfort from "corporate boxes" leased to companies for the purposes of entertaining business visitors. In addition, there are the more cultural forms of entertainment such as the theatre and opera, and the less cultural forms of entertainment such as bars, casinos and cabarets.

Business Meetings

At business meetings, Australians like to get things done—some other cultures might think—with great haste. The first action at a meeting is usually the exchange of business cards. Business people mostly address one another by their first names, although there are exceptions.

A series of preliminary meetings to allow participants to get to know one another is not the Australian way. Generally, it is down to business right away. Meetings are likely to be democratic and sometimes even unruly. All present are likely to contribute to the discussion at hand, although meetings occasionally include observers who report the proceedings to parties not in attendance.

Most meetings operate more or less to common rules of protocol, where comments are directed through the meeting convenor and minutes of important meetings are normally kept to ensure all parties understand what has been agreed on.

Working with Staff

The performance of the workforce is driven by many factors. The office culture that the employer establishes is an important factor within the employer's control. Performance is enhanced if employees derive satisfaction from the job they are doing. Most Australian workers do not like the boss to monopolise all the good ideas. On the contrary, usually motivated by good intentions, Australian workers are prepared to strike on their own to make their own improvements. Australians tend to develop a wide range of skills outside their speciality.

Australians excel in the area of individual pursuits. They make excellent test pilots, mountain climbers, Antarctic explorers and round-the-world sailors. When it comes to innovation, they sometimes need to be restrained rather than encouraged. However, such independence of spirit may not always work all that well in a team environment and needs to be controlled.

To get the best out of a workforce, an employer should consider creating an environment where employees' suggestions can be heard, considered and discussed. A democratic style of management, where the workforce is involved in the decision making, is likely to be successful and is widely practised.

Whether Australians work for a foreign company or an Australian-owned company is not normally an issue in employee relations. What an Australian employee values most is having the adequate resources to accomplish his task, a clear understanding of the employer's expectations and a comfortable relationship with his or her fellow employees. Like people everywhere, Australians do not enjoy being criticised. However, formal appraisal of work performance, usually involving a mixture of criticism and praise, is a normal part of the employment contract of most people.

Australians are not particularly good at hiding their feelings. You will be able to read the morale of the workforce merely by observing their physical behaviour and body language. Should you become interested enough to ask them what is on their minds, nine out of ten Australians will tell you exactly what the problem is—especially if it is you.

In the Community

Most business visitors stay at hotels, of which a wide range is available—including the international chains found in most countries. Travelling beyond the environs of the hotel is unrestricted. Australia is one of the safest countries in which to wander at will in the street.

Birdsville, Australia's most remote town, is situated in the Simpson Desert. The mere act of travelling here is considered a pioneering event.

Getting Around

Taxis are converted sedan cars, readily available and easily identifiable. In Victoria, all taxis have a gold and black check distinguishing mark down their sides.

If you sit beside the driver, be prepared to engage in a conversation with him. Cab drivers in Australia tend to be philosophers. Unlike some other places in the world, they are more likely to discuss with you the state of the world than talk up the fare or set up dates between you and their close friends.

All taxis use meters based on an initial charge ('the flagfall") and a kilometre rate. This saves you the exhausting process of negotiating a rate for a journey of unknown length and duration.

Getting around in cabs is reasonably inexpensive and easier than using public transport systems, which are not particularly user friendly, with the exception of airport buses. Even experienced users may find travelling on public transport difficult in the major cities when they stray from their accustomed route. Public transport systems are generally uninformative about routes, the correct platforms and the location of ticket sellers.

You can, of course, get around Australia in your own hired car. While Australians are for the most part laid-back, when they get behind the wheel of a car, a significant percentage of them suffer a personality change. A recent phenomenon is "road rage" where drivers get beaten up by their fellow road users for perceived discourtesies on the road. If you are driving and see another driver emerge from his or her car and advance in your direction, keep the window up and the door locked. No incident has yet been reported where drivers have resorted to shooting each other.

Shopping

Shopping in Australian cities is a blend of old and new. Large department stores and strip shopping—where individual shops cluster along roadways—are found in the main city precincts, while the more recently constructed large shopping centres are located further out of the city. In addition, there are a few markets where goods are sold from stalls.

Australians have inherited the English tradition of forming orderly queues in situations where more than one person is waiting for the same service.[3] Self-service shopping, which originated in supermarkets, has spread to most forms of retailing. In some shops, an assistant may offer help to shoppers who look bewildered but for the most part, shoppers must take the initiative if they want help. In large shops, prices are generally not negotiable. In smaller shops, where the proprietor of the shop may be within easy reach, the shopkeeper may sometimes be persuaded to lower the price.

Tipping

Tipping is not as widespread as it once was. In the past, tipping in restaurants was almost mandatory, regardless of the service provided. Now, customers are more discerning. Not every restaurant waiter gets a tip these days despite the fact that the standard of service has probably risen as a result of the influx of tourists to most parts of the country.

People you should tip include the doormen and bellhops in your hotel, and anyone else in the hotel who can help make your stay comfortable. People who expect tips in some countries but not in Australia are taxi drivers and hairdressers. It is probably advisable to tip waiters in restaurants provided the service rendered was acceptable. Restaurant tips are about 10%. Hotel staff can be given the odd one or two dollar coins.

Smoking

Smoking in Australia is becoming ever more restricted. The smoking ban started with the internal airlines and spread to most forms of transportation, then invaded office blocks. Wandering through the city, you will probably observe groups of people in the street hanging around doorways of office blocks smoking. These people are not out-of-work layabouts but office workers who have "ducked downstairs for a smoko". Smoking is still allowed in the streets but if you do smoke, be careful about the way you dispose of the butt. Littering may cost a $100 on-the-spot fine.

In restaurants, smokers find themselves herded into smaller and smaller areas. Some restaurants have banned smoking completely. Others quarantine smokers into unwanted corners of the restaurant, often near the kitchen. Smokers dying to light up in someone's home but unsure if smoking is in order, are advised to head for the back garden. There, you will most likely encounter a group of fellow exiles with at least one common interest.

According to health department statistics, 25% of the population are smokers and 80% of those who do smoke want to quit. Government revenue taken from smokers as excise duty is $4 billion per annum versus health department estimates of $12 billion per annum treating tobacco-related illnesses.

Women in Society

With the decline in real wages over the last decade and a half, many women have returned or attempted to return to the workforce to supplement the family income. In a typical household of the 1940s, 1950s and 1960s, the husband was the sole breadwinner. Now, for marriages where the wife is less than 50 years old, 64% of wives have jobs, while many others work on a casual or part-time basis.

Equal opportunity legislation precludes discrimination against employees on the grounds of gender, race and physical handicap. However, these principles are difficult to enforce. Despite theoretical equality of the sexes, most of the top positions in the industries are still occupied by men. However, women do dominate in some industries such as publishing and fashion: industries that turn out products of which women are the largest consumers.

One of the areas in which women are not doing well, at least statistically, is the boardroom, where only 4% of company directors are women. Women are doing better in politics, however, where about 20% of the sitting members are women (compared to a global average of 13%) and about the same percent are ministers (compared to a global average of 6%).

No woman has yet made prime minister or leader of the opposition. However, two women, Janine Haines and Cheryl Curnot, have led the Democrats at different times. Other women leaders include Joan Kirner from Victoria and Dr. Carmen Lawrence from Western Australia.

Dr. Carmen Lawrence, who was the most decorated student across all faculties in her 1968 graduating class of the University of Western Australia, moved to federal parliament and became the Minister of Health in the Keating Labor government where she earned a reputation of being the best debater in parliament. Dr. Lawrence could probably have become leader of the opposition after Keating's team lost the 1996 election. From here, she would most likely have stood a good chance of becoming the first female

Australian prime minister. However, she fell victim to a Liberal Party-inspired political witch hunt to remove talent from the Labor front benches and is no longer a political force.

First Woman in Parliament

The first woman elected to an Australian Parliament was Edith Cowan, who was elected to the parliament of Western Australia in 1921. In her maiden speech, the new member immediately tackled the main issue of the day—that a woman had to pay an extra shilling if she wanted to bring a pram into the train. Edith Cowan took exception to this surcharge, suggesting that the Minister for Railways should suffer from his own policy by parading the streets of Perth for an entire afternoon with a heavy child on one arm and a bag of groceries on the other.

Edith Cowan's portrait appears on the back of the Australian $5 note today—an acknowledgement of her contribution to women's issues.

The most talked about woman in Australian politics, Pauline Hanson, is Australia's most prominent redneck. This is a role few woman would want, but the fact that she is a woman is really not a factor within the Australian community. Public perception of Pauline Hanson comes from her policies, not her gender.

Under Paul Keating, the Labor government declared an intention to institute a policy that the proportion of female candidates should reflect the proportion of women in the community. This was rejected by women's groups as tokenism. Women of this mindset demanded that the best candidates be nominated regardless of gender.

Recent studies in education have shown that female students in secondary education outperform males. Moreover, girls have departed from their traditionally perceived roles of being good at arts but poor at science. Girls are winning the prizes in the so called hard disciplines of mathematics and physics as well as

The His/Herstory of Sexist Language

Laws have been passed to eliminate sexist language in the documents of the Australian Public Service. To this end, an entire section of the public service was appointed to the task of identifying gender specific words and making appropriate substitutions. Thus "chairmen" became "chairpersons" and "manholes" became "utility access holes". The use of "he" to mean an unspecified person was also replaced by "he/she" and "his/hers".

At times, this process attracted its critics as it made government documents, such as tender documents and government bills, very clumsy. As an exasperated "Letter to the Editor" in *The Australian* protested, "surely we can redefine the term *man* in this context to mean 'man as embracing woman…!'"

maintaining their stranglehold on the humanities. The only group in Australian education who, on aggregate, outscore the girls are the Asian children who exceed the population average. However, even in the Asian households, girls get a better rating than boys. The best performing sub-group of the entire Australian secondary education system is Chinese females.

Sociologists have recently become alarmed at the employment prospects of youths who do badly at school, in particular those who are unable to get tertiary qualifications. The spectre of youth unemployment, running at 40% in some areas, looms as one of the country's largest problems in the future.

Superstition, Luck and Gambling

Superstition and luck are not generally thought to play a part in business negotiations. Fridays falling on the 13th day of the month (an event that occurs either once or twice per year) are considered unlucky days by a few superstitious diehards. A significant number of people believe in astrology but such people are mainly outside the business circle. The mysterious astrological forces are mainly

On safari, but still keeping up with schoolwork. Recent studies have shown that female students outperform their male counterparts.

thought to influence personal relationships. Astrological charts are usually found in women's magazines and tabloid newspapers.

There are no lucky or unlucky colours in mainstream Anglo-Saxon culture. However this does not apply to everyone. Melbourne's vast Crown Casino, built in the hope of attracting high rollers from Asia, decorated a substantial part of its high stakes room in gold and red—colours that the Chinese consider lucky.

While Australians are not particularly superstitious, they spend a lot of time and money gambling, betting an average of about $800 per head in 1996—or about 3% of average income. The nationwide gambling market turnover in 1996 was $10.6 billion.[4]

Tradition has it that Australians would bet "on two flies crawling up a wall." In this vein, Australians invented the game "two up", an absurdly simple betting game which can be played

The Melbourne Crown Casino

The Melbourne Crown Casino was an incredibly controversial project. The casino was promoted by Victoria's Liberal premier, Jeff Kennett, the most rambunctious state premier since the days of Queensland's Sir Joh Bjelke-Petersen. The casino licence was generally regarded as a licence to print money in gambling-mad, casino-starved Victoria. When the project was mooted, 22 potential bidders from around the world expressed interest.

The successful applicant, the Crown Consortium, included as its major shareholders, the treasurer of the Victorian Liberal Party, personal friends of the premier and other Liberal Party benefactors. The award of the casino licence was criticised by Victoria's auditor general on the grounds that Crown did not submit the highest complying bid for the licence and may have received inside information on the details of competitive bids.

The federal Senate moved to investigate into the casino tendering process but this was frustrated by the combined forces of the state and federal Liberal governments.

Crime authorities claim that the casino is a centre for money laundering and drug dealing. Community groups representing Asian immigrants, who make up a large percentage of casino patrons, claim that Melbourne ethnic communities have been devastated since the casino commenced its operations.

with almost no equipment and requires no more than two players. To play "two up", two coins will be tossed simultaneously, which will land either "odds" (head and a tail) or "evens" (two heads or two tails). The odds are, of course, 50/50 for each outcome.

Over the last decade, competition for the gambling dollar has intensified. Australians have invested vast sums of money betting on horse and greyhound races, which are major but declining industries. Additional gambling outlets, particularly poker machines, have taken revenue from track races.

Gambling regulations vary from state to state. In the 1950s and 1960s, states like New South Wales spawned an entire subculture of "sporting clubs" financed from the takings of poker machines. Previously, frustrated gamblers of more conservative states like Victoria, where poker machines were banned, would book tour buses to towns on the New South Wales border to spend the day and considerable sums of money "at the pokies".

The range of gambling outlets has increased since then. Australia's first casino was a modest but tasteful affair built in Tasmania in the 1960s as an adjunct to Hobart's Wrest Point Hotel. This has been followed by larger gaming houses as the different states competed with one another for the gambling dollar. Casinos were built in Launceston, Adelaide, Perth, Surfer's Paradise and Sydney, culminating in the largest of them all—Melbourne's $2.3 billion Crown Casino, which covers approximately four city blocks and is reputedly the second largest casino in the world. After a late start, Melbourne entered the gambling world with a vengeance.

Conclusion

Australia's free and easy lifestyle spills over into business. While you will be expected to display a modicum of social grace, business success is related primarily to the activities conducted within the four walls of your office. As a foreigner to Australia, you are more likely to find yourself welcomed than discriminated against.

Australia is a fine country in which to set up a business venture. There are plenty of people willing to lend a hand to make your business successful: the government in its many layers, the skilled workforce, eager customers, providers of infrastructure, and ethnic and other business networks. Australians like to see businesses succeed. Few people in Australia are admired as much as a foreign settler who makes good.

Good luck!

Basic Facts and Travel Tips

Climate

The state of Queensland—Australia's most popular tourist destination—advertises its weather to be "beautiful one day and perfect the next".

Broadly speaking, Australia's climate is tropical in the areas north of Brisbane (the capital of Queensland) and temperate in the areas south of Brisbane. Weather in the tropical areas is sticky in summer, and warm and pleasant for the other months. Weather in the temperate areas is warm and hot in summer, and cool and wet in winter.

The winters are not as cold as that in Europe or Canada, although sufficient snow falls on high ground during winter in the "Australian Alps" of Victoria and New South Wales to support a skiing industry. In summer, all the main centres can get very hot, even Hobart, which is the most southerly of the capital cities.

One thing to remember about Australia is that the seasons are the reverse of the Northern Hemisphere—summer runs from December to February and winter starts in June and ends in August.

Crime and Drugs

Like most societies, Australia has experienced an increasing number of drug addicts in recent years. Theft of property has also increased commensurately. Most criminologists believe that drug use and theft are linked—people are stealing to support their drug habit. However, out and out mugging is uncommon in Australia. You are more likely to be relieved of your possessions through sleight of hand than brute force. It is still relatively safe to walk around at night in most areas.

Travellers to Australia should take care to supervise their public property. Petty thieves will target anything that can be easily turned into cash. Leading the list are wallets and handbags. Another favourite target is mobile phones, particularly those left within plain sight on the seat of a parked car—where more damage will be done to the car than the value of the phone. Another favourite target is RAM computer chips which can be advertised in the local *Trading Post*—a newspaper which advertises for the exchange and sales of items—and readily turned into cash. Notepad PCs such as a business person might carry are particularly desirable to thieves, as are high value, easily tradeable items like cameras.

Currency

The Australian currency is the Australian dollar, known within the country as the "dollar" or "the buck". In the financial press, the Australian dollar is called the AUD or even the "Aussie" to distinguish it from the many other dollars of global commerce. The minor unit is the cent—one hundredth part of a dollar— which has so little buying power that one cent and two cent coins were recently withdrawn from circulation.

Coinage in circulation is five, 10, 20 and 50 cents plus one and two dollars. Notes in circulation are five, 10, 20, 50 and 100 dollars. Some years ago, Australia introduced the world's first plastic bank note (to replace paper notes as the plastic notes last much longer in circulation). Today, Australia is gradually moving towards a cashless society, with more and more financial transactions being performed electronically.

Customs and Excise

Flora and fauna are fragile. Imported species of plants and animals tend to run riot once introduced. Since settlement, Australia has imported plant and animal pests that are now totally out of control. These pests include rabbits, cane toads, cats, foxes, European carp, thistles and brambles. To avoid repeating such mistakes, Australia has strict prohibitions on organic imports. Exotic species of animals and plants are allowed to enter only under strict provisions. Animals such as horses and dogs are subject to quarantine restrictions. Packing cases made from organic material such as timber must be appropriately treated with fumigating agents. Even people are sprayed with insecticide on arrival in the country!

Australia is a signatory to international agreements seeking to prevent the laundering of drug money. Thus import and export of large quantities of cash of all currencies is restricted and has to be declared. No more than $10,000 may be imported or exported as cash though monetary transfers through banks are not restricted. Other restricted exports and imports include dangerous or antisocial goods such as weapons and poisons.

Dates and Time

The European date system is pretty much standard in the country. Thus, 1 January 1997 is written as 6/1/1997 and 1 June 1997 is written 1/6/97.

The country has three official time zones operating in the different states. They are outlined below.

Eastern Standard Time (EST) is 10 hours ahead of Greenwich Mean Time (GMT). EST operates in New South Wales, Victoria, Queensland and Tasmania.

Central Time applies to South Australia and Northern Territory and is half an hour behind EST, that is nine and a half hours ahead of GMT.

Western Australian Time is two hours behind EST, or eight hours ahead of GMT.

On top of that, some people in the eastern half of Western Australia set clocks to their own time called "Gold Fields Time", which is halfway between Western Time and Central Time

This guide is reliable for winter which runs from about mid-March to mid-October. However, in summer, rules of time vary between the states. Sentiment on summer time is split between farmers, who don't like it, and the rest of the community who do. States whose governments are excessively influenced by the agricultural lobby, such as Western Australia and Queensland, do not have summer time at all. The other states put their clocks forward one hour. (Summer time in Victoria, NSW and Tasmania thus becomes GMT plus 11 hours, while Queensland time remains GMT plus 10 hours and Western Australian time remains GMT plus eight hours.)

In addition, Victoria and New South Wales start and end their summer time at different dates so that in the second week in March, Victoria may be on summer time while New South Wales has commenced winter time.

Australia's inability to operate a national policy on summer time creates endless confusion within the country, particularly with airline schedules. If you are travelling interstate in summer, double check your bookings so that you don't arrive one hour early at the airport or worse, one hour late!

Electricity, Television and Video Standards
Voltage at point of use is 240 v 50 Hz single phase, or 415 v 50 Hz three phase. For large installations, 6000 v 50 Hz or more can be available on negotiation.

For domestic use, flat three pin plugs are used throughout the country. The existing plugs on your appliances will probably have to be replaced since the Australian plug is different from that of most countries. Wire fuses are common in domestic installations, while breakers are commonly used in commercial installations.

Power boards in common use domestically and commercially also incorporate separate overload protection.

The battle of the video player technologies was won by VHS, using the European PAL system. Video recorders will play NTSC tapes but the quality of PAL tapes is far superior. Almost all homes and most offices in Australia have a video tape recorder. It is therefore not worth bringing a video recorder since getting access to one is not difficult. Tapes in PAL and NTSC formats brought in from overseas are likely to work satisfactorily.

Like almost any country, computers are widely used.

Geography

Australia is the world's second driest continent—only Antarctica is drier. For this reason, only one-third of the country is permanently inhabited. Despite its size, Australia's population is only 18 million—less than that of California.

The heaviest rain falls on the fertile farming areas around the eastern and southern coastlines, the tropical north, and on the island state of Tasmania. The south-west corner of Western Australian also receives good winter rains. The majority of the population lives in these areas.

Australia's main mountain group is the Great Dividing Range, which runs the entire 2,500 mile length of the east coast. On the opposite side of the continent is the low lying Kimberley Range on the north-west coast.

The longest river in Australia is the Murray, which has several important tributaries, notably the Darling and Murrumbidgee Rivers. The Murray Darling system, as the complex of rivers is known, drains about a seventh of the continent, carrying rainfall off the western slopes of the Great Dividing Range to the interior of the country. For over 100 years, this natural drainage basin has been extensively irrigated for crops. Despite its large catchment area, flow in the Murray Darling system is not large. The annual flow of the Murray-Darling system is less than the daily flow of the Amazon.

Some people call the desert in the centre of the country the "Dead Heart" of Central Australia where, under a relentless sun, the red mulga plains roll to an endless horizon.

Australia's Geography at a Glance

Highest Mountain	Mount Kosciusko (2,228m)
Lowest Point	Lake Eyre (Salt Lake), (15.24 m below sea level
Coastline	19,650 km
Longest River	Murray-Darling Rivers (3,600 km)
Northernmost Point	Cape York, Queensland
Southernmost Point	South Cape, Tasmania
Westernmost Point	Steep Point, Western Australia
Easternmost Point	Cape Byron, NSW
Hottest Temperature	59° C—Bourke NSW—17 January 1877
Coldest Temperature	Minus 25° C—Charlotte Pass NSW—14 July 1945
Terrain	Mostly plains country. Low mountain range along the eastern seaboard. The mean elevation of 200 m is the lowest of any continent.
Land Use	6% under cultivation 14% tropical or temperate forest 47% sandy plains and desert Balance—grasslands or urban areas
National Animals	Emu and Kangaroo
National Flower	The wattle—gold flower and green leaves—national colours.
National Tree	The gum tree (eucalyptus)

Hotels

Tourism has boomed in Australia over the past decade, with a commensurate boom in hotel construction. A full range of accommodation exists in all major capital cities and also in the major tourist resorts. Room occupancy rates have generally been high in recent years as the number of available beds has only just kept ahead of demand.

For quality city accommodation, it pays to book ahead. In the provincial areas, motels are the common form of accommodation and are in abundant supply, so no advance booking is needed. Motels are cheap and adequate, but have minimal services. Most do not have dining rooms, though breakfast can be brought to your room when requested. Virtually all hotels and motels are fully self contained with en suite bathroom facilities, televisions, refrigerators and air conditioning.

Immigration and Visa Requirements

The objective of Australia's immigration programme is to import sufficient immigrants to satisfy a mix of social and political objectives. About 50% of migrants are family members wishing to reunite with those already living in Australia. The economic objectives of the other 50% are to bring in people with the means or particular skills for business.

Australia allocates each overseas country a quota that establishes the number of migrants Australia is prepared to take. Those interested in settling in Australia by participating in the migration programme should contact the Department of Immigration to establish the immigration arrangements for the particular country.

Visa requirements for short term visits have been relaxed in recent years. However, it would be wise to consult your travel agent or the Australian Consulate in your country before going to the country.

Matters of Interest to Visitors to Australia

Health Regulations	No health certificate required unless the traveller is over 70 years old
Visa Requirements	Varies with situation. Check with the local consulate
Airport Tax	Departure tax of $27
Driving Licence	International licence acceptable for up to 12 months. After that, a local licence is required.
Local Currency	Money laundering provisions restrict export of Australian dollars conveyed as cash
Use of Credit Cards	All well-known credit cards are widely used
Money Changer	Most banks
Power Supply	240 v 50 Hz—single phase 415 v 50 Hz—3 phase to industrial areas

Public Holidays in Australia

Public holidays vary slightly between the states. Those celebrated in all the states include:

- New Year's Day — 1 January
- Australia Day — 26 January
- Good Friday — March/April—date varies
- Easter Monday — March/April—date varies

- Anzac Day	25 April
- Queen's Birthday	9 June
- Christmas	25 December
- Boxing Day	26 December

Public Holidays celebrated in certain states include:

- Labour Day	Varies between states
- Melbourne Cup Day	First Tuesday in November
	(Victoria only)
- Show Day	October—date varies
- Foundation Day	2 June (Western Australia)

Schools
Seventy percent of Australian students attend government-run schools and 30% attend private schools. Examination results of private schools are significantly better than public schools, and a higher proportion of their secondary graduates go for tertiary education. Education standards are about equivalent to those in the UK. School curriculum in Australia is in the English language, although private specialist foreign language schools are available in the major capital cities.

Shopping Hours
Shopping hours used to be restricted. In fact, in 1985, a Victorian hardware shop proprietor was sent to jail for persistently opening his shop on Sundays. However, in recent years, such legislated restrictions have all but disappeared.

Shopping hours vary. Many shops operate at hours that suit them while shopping hours in malls are imposed by landlords. Other shops open on all sorts of timetables, with some open 24 hours a day, seven days a week.

Travelling inside Australia

Australia has a well-developed road system and an extensive internal air network. The interstate rail system has never really overcome the problem of different track gauges in the states. While suburban rail networks exist in most cities to take commuters to and from work, long distance rail has never been developed to the extent of the rail systems in Europe. The infrequent interstate trains are slow, uncomfortable and expensive. Most people prefer to travel by air or road.

Travelling to Australia

Australia has nine international airports. Kingsford-Smith Airport in Sydney handles the largest number of passengers . The greatest amount of freight is handled by Tullamarine Airport in Melbourne. The other international airports are in Brisbane, Perth, Adelaide, Darwin, Hobart, Canberra and Cairns.

Directory of Important Contacts

Australian Bureau of Agricultural and Resource Economics (ABARE)
Edmund Barton Building
Cnr Broughton &
Macquarie St
Barton ACT 2601
GPO Box 1563 Canberra
ACT 2601
Tel: (06) 272 2000
Fax: (06) 272 2001

Australian Bureau of Statistics (ABS)
St Andrews House
Sydney Square, Sydney
2001, NSW *or*
GPO Box 796, Sydney,
NSW, 2001
Tel: (008) 221 077
Fax: (02) 268 4599

Reserve Bank of Australia (RBA)
65 Martin Place
Sydney NSW 2000
Tel: (02) 9551 9721
Fax: (02) 9551 8000

Austrade
PO Box 55 World Trade
Centre
Melbourne, Victoria 3000
or
21st Floor 40 City Road
South Melbourne, Victoria
3205
Tel: 13 2878
Fax: (03) 9284 3000
Internet:
http://www.austrade.gov.au

Export Finance and Insurance Corporation (EFIC)
Level 20, 40 City Road,
South Melbourne, Victoria
3205
PO Box 38, Flinders Lane,
Melbourne, Victoria, 8009
Tel: (03) 9206 4900
Fax: (03) 9206 4914

Australian Marketing Institute
Level 2, 464 St Kilda Road,
South Melbourne, Victoria,
3004
Tel: (03) 9820 8788
Fax: (03) 9820 8650

Directory of Australian Associations National Guide to Government
75 Flinders Lane,
Melbourne, Victoria, 3000
Tel: (03) 9654 2800
Fax: (03) 9654 2800
e-mail: info.aust.com.au
Internet: editor.aust.com.au

List of Lists
(One stop list of all government departments)
Level 10, 227 Collins St.,
Melbourne, Victoria 3000
Tel: 1800 060 555
Fax: (03) 9629 7878
e-mail:
bookman@ozemail.com.au

Australian Customs Service (ACS)
5-11 Constitution Drive,
Canberra, ACT 2601
Tel: 1300 363 263
Fax: (06) 275 6059
Internet: http://www.customs.gov.au

Department of Industry, Science and Tourism
20 Allara St., Canberra,
ACT 2601
Tel: (06) 213 6000
Fax: (06) 275 6213

Australian Competition and Consumer Commission
PO Box 19, Belconnen,
ACT, 2606
Tel: (06) 264 1166
Internet:
http://www.accc.gov.au

Australian Securities Commission
5th Floor, 15 London Circuit, Canberra, ACT, 2601
Tel: (06) 250 3850
Internet: http://www.asc.gov.au

Office of National Tourism
Level 4, 20 Allara St.
Canberra, ACT, 2601
Tel: (02) 6213 7124
Fax: (02) 6213 6983
e-mail:
bureau.tourism.research
@dist.gov.au

Australian Chamber of Manufacturers
380 St Kilda Road, South
Melbourne, Victoria, 3004
Tel: 1800 331 103
Fax: (03) 9699 1729

Retail Traders Association
104 Franklin St.,
Melbourne, Victoria, 3000
Tel: (03) 9326 5022
Internet:
HBIA@RTAV.com.au

Australian Taxation Office
Tel:13 2860
Internet:
http://www.ato.gov.au

Information Australia
75 Flinders Lane,
Melbourne, Victoria, 3000
Tel: (03) 9654 2800
Fax: (03) 9650 5261

R & D AusIndustry Hotline
20 Allara St., Canberra,
ACT, 2601
Tel: 13 28 46
Internet:
http://www.dist.gov.au

CSIRO
PO Box 225, Dixon,
ACT 2602
Limestone Avenue,
Canberra, ACT, 2601
Tel: 1800 645 7555
Fax: (03) 9662 7555
Internet: http://www.csiro.au

Stock Exchange
580 Collins St., Melbourne,
Victoria, 3000
Tel: 1300 300 279
Internet:
http://www.asx.com.au
Australian Stock Exchange
Listing Rules - available for
$75, plus $75 for one year's
upgrades, if required. For
copies, phone Australian
Stock Exchange.

Companies Express
4th Floor, 18 Queen St.,
Melbourne, Victoria, 3000
Tel: (03) 9629 7300
Fax: (03) 9629 8137
Internet:
http://www.compex.com.au

Australian Institute of Management
181 Fitzroy St. St. Kilda,
Victoria, 3182
Tel: (03) 9534 8181
Internet:
http://www.aim.com.au

Further Reading

Donald Horne. *The Lucky Country Revisited*. Melbourne: Dent, 1987.
An update of the 1960s definitive text on Australian business and social culture. Easy reading

Rob Connelly & Peter Rock. *Managing Australian Business*. Sydney: McMillan, 1995.
A textbook style treatise on Australian business writing in free and easy to read style.

Price Waterhouse. *Doing Business in Australia*. Florida, USA: Price Waterhouse, 1994.
A handbook on Australian tax and accounting practice. While fairly formal in style, it has been designed to be easy to read. Useful for those setting up a business in Australia

Australian Department of the Environment. *Report on the Environment—Executive Summary*. Victoria, Australia: CSIRO, Collingwood, 1996.
A readable report on the state of the environment, available free of charge from the Department of the Environment

John Buss & Graham Herford. *Personal Selling in Australia*. Sydney: McGraw Hill, 1994.
While a formal textbook, there is some material which may be of interest to those setting up a company to manufacture and market consumer products within Australia

Notes

Chapter 1

1. The Organisation of Economic Cooperation and Development (OECD) is based in Paris. Countries in this group include Australia, Austria, Belgium/Luxembourg, Canada, Czechoslovakia, Denmark, Finland, France, Germany, Greece, Iceland, Ireland, Italy, Japan, Korea, Mexico, Norway, Portugal, Spain, Sweden, Switzerland, Turkey, United Kingdom and United States.
2. On the other hand, countries like Japan, which were rebuilt after the Second World War, grew at 8% GNP per capita per annum for a long period—thereby raising the global average growth rate. Once the Japanese economy had grown to its present maturity, the growth rate declined. Comparing the growth rates of already mature economies with a global average that includes developing economies is probably not very useful.
3. In 1995, the GATT nations renamed their organisation the World Trade Organisation (WTO).
4. "Banana Republic" describes an economy that relies on exporting a single commodity (the figurative banana), the price of which is set by importing countries. The derogatory term was using to disparage Australia's economic dependence on a few commodities exported by the primary sector.
5. Loans and equity invested in Australia by overseas lenders and investors minus loans and equity invested overseas by Australian lenders and investors.
6. Average hours worked per week in May 1997 was 35.7 compared to 35.6 for the period 1983 to 1984.

Chapter 2

1. Measured at average 1989-90 prices
2. These are the National Bank of Australia, the Commonwealth Bank, Westpac and the Australia New Zealand Bank.
3. These are accounts paying a certain minimum level of interest.

Chapter 3

1. This alliance became disparagingly known by the name "WA Inc."
2. The prominent advocate was Jeffery Kennett, the premier of Victoria.
3. In fact, it was reintroduced, having historically been imposed then abolished.

Chapter 5

1. The value of one Australian dollar (A$) in 1965 was US$1.50. By the 1990s, this rate had halved to around A$1 = US$ 0.75.

Chapter 6

1. Like British Law, Australian law is generously studded with phrases in the Latin language.

Chapter 7

1. So far as can be established, no one consulted the teeming hordes to check out how they would have felt about living in an Australian desert.
2. The Torres Straight Islands that come under Australian jurisdiction are, as their name suggest, islands in the Torres Straight, the expanse of seawater between Australia and Papua New Guinea.
3. Each year, the monthly business magazine *Business Review Weekly* compiles a list of the 200 richest people in Australia.
4. Somewhat miraculously, this destitute's son, John Bond, is presently one of the richest people in the country.
5. *Chooks*, in Australian English, is the term for farmyard chickens.
6. Bourke is the most westerly town in New South Wales. "Back of Bourke" is the general description for the desolate country of the outback. Other terms for the same region are "Beyond the Black Stump" and the "Never Never".

Chapter 8

1. This response is correct for males only. There is no known female equivalent.
2. "Grace" is the Christian pre-dinner blessing to thank The Lord for providing the food on the table.
3. Australians are not quite as assiduous as the British, of whom it is said that two people meeting casually in the street will form a queue merely to keep in practice.
4. The 1996 gambling dollar was split—48.4% poker machines, 17.9% racing, 16.8% casinos, and 12.6% lotteries.

About the Authors

An Australian citizen, PETER NORTH is a graduate of Melbourne University with degrees in engineering and economics. He began his career in an engineering design office before branching out to construction projects in the United Kingdom and the Middle East, and mining projects in Australia, South Africa and Papua New Guinea. He was later involved in various manufacturing ventures in Australia and Thailand. While in the Middle East, he lectured an MBA course on business statistics and mathematics at the Golden Gate University. He later lectured in business finance at Bradford University in Thailand. His other published work is *Countries of the World: Australia* (Times Editions).

BEA TOEWS was born in Canada where she obtained her Bachelors degree in Arts and Education. She later migrated to Australia and completed her Masters in Education and Business. Since then, she has taught in schools and colleges in Canada, Australia and Thailand, managed a restaurant and several bookshops in Australia, and written business and executive English programmes for a bank and a research institute in Thailand. Her other published work is *Succeed in Business: Thailand* (Times Editions).

Index